You and Your Assets

You and Your Assets

A Practical Guide to Financial Management and Estate Planning

Martin R. Dunetz

MADISON BOOKS
Lanham • New York • Oxford

Published by Madison Books
4720 Boston Way
Lanham, Maryland 20706

12 Hid's Copse Road
Cummor Hill, Oxford OX2 9JJ, England

Dunetz, Martin R.
    You and your assets : a practical guide to financial management
and estate planning / Martin R. Dunetz.
        p. cm.
    Includes index.
    ISBN 1-56833-091-X (alk. paper)
    1. Finance, Personal. 2. Estate planning. 3. Tax planning.
4. Mutual funds. I. Title.
HG179.D855 1997
332.024—dc21   96-52480
                                                                    CIP

ISBN 1–56833–091–X (cloth : alk. paper)

Distributed by National Book Network

⊖™ The paper used in this publication meets the minimum requirements of
American National Standard for Information Sciences—Permanence of
Paper for Printed Library Materials, ANSI Z39.48–1984.
Manufactured in the United States of America.

To Marta

"Anyone may so arrange his affairs that his taxes shall be as low as possible; he is not bound to choose that pattern which will best pay the Treasury. There is not even a patriotic duty to increase one's taxes."

—Honorable Learned Hand

Disclaimer

This book was written with the intention of providing accurate information on various subjects, including wills, trusts, investments, and financial and retirement planning. It is printed, sold, or distributed with the understanding that neither the author, the publisher, nor the one who markets the book is engaged in providing legal, accounting, insurance, investment, tax, financial, retirement, or other professional advice. Before following any suggestions proposed or implied in this book, the reader is urged to seek an expert in the particular field in which advice is sought. Additionally, because of possible or unanticipated changes in governing statutes and tax and case law relating to the application of any information contained in this book, the author, the publisher, and any and all persons or entities involved in any way in the preparation, publication, sale, or distribution of this book disclaim all responsibility for the legal effects or consequences of any document prepared or action taken in reliance upon information, figures, or illustrations contained in this book. No representations, either express or implied, are made or given regarding the legal consequences of this book. Purchasers and persons intending to use this book for the preparation of any legal documents are advised to check specifically on the current applicable laws in any jurisdiction in which they intend the documents to be effective.

Contents

Acknowledgment

I would like to thank Donald Earl Williamson, Jr., B.S., M.A., M.Div., for the word processing skills he exhibited during the construction of this book.

1

The Need and Purpose of Estate Planning: What It Is and How It Can Help You . . . An Introduction

Someone once said, "There are two systems of taxation in our country: one for the informed and one for the uninformed." If this is true, and I believe most people will agree that it is, then a book to introduce you to some of the tax-savings techniques of a "broadened" view of estate planning should be welcome. This book goes well beyond a discussion of wills and trusts and deals with asset protection, personal trust management, and investment strategies as they relate to your estate both current and into the future. Its overall purpose is to bring estate planning down to a practical level and to make some sense out of a discipline that is generally confined to the "law" and to lawyers. The book is directed, then, to those of you with inquiring minds who wish to familiarize yourselves with some of the terms, methods, and techniques involved in making premortem transfers to loved ones and to establish provisions you would like realized and made effective after your death. Doing this without paying more taxes than one is legally obligated to pay is what this book is about.

Estate planning is not merely for the wealthy. With the

value of homes and other undervalued and overlooked assets having increased substantially over the years, many people who would not have been subject to estate tax duties in the past will now have to pay their fair share. These assets may also include among others, your life insurance proceeds, investment securities monies from jointly held properties, bank accounts, farmland and other real estate, such as your home and stamp and coin collections that were forgotten and are still in the attic. With a burgeoning federal deficit that cries out for more revenue from any likely source, you, perhaps with the help of your spouse, must try to protect your assets while you are alive and make provisions for your survivor(s) after your death. The disposition of your estate, if not properly planned, can be particularly burdensome to those who are left behind without a plan and not knowing what to do or how to deal with the problem. Losing a loved one "who took care of things" can be extremely difficult financially, and it can be emotionally draining if you are the one who will have to deal with creditors, lawyers, accountants, an insurance company, perhaps a real estate agent, and federal and state governments.

Death taxes, both federal and state, are not the only obstacle the surviving spouse will be confronted with. There are settlement costs that have to be paid which consist primarily of probate expenses and other administrative fees. Probate costs are generally paid to the executor of the estate and the attorney who assists with the probate process. If an estate does not have sufficient assets in liquid form to pay settlement costs or if there is not enough current income to care for a spouse and/or minor children, not only will it be stressful, but it will cause deep financial hurt to those left behind. Having some liquidity is most important because transferring assets into an appropriate beneficiary's name so each may receive income, can be subject to probate delays and expenses. Other problems can also arise. For example, assets that may have to be transferred to minors may have to be in guardianship or custodian accounts until the minors reach age twenty-one. Important and necessary records can be misplaced. Stock certificates may be incorrectly titled, real estate holdings or shares of stock, because of market conditions, may be severely reduced in value and required to be sold at capital losses, and important papers, such as a deed to your home, cannot be found and must be replaced. Unfortunately, most people do little record keeping or planning in this regard and allow their beneficiaries to worry about any problems that may arise when it is too late. It is especially troublesome when the Internal Revenue Service comes knocking on your door requesting its share of the estate in the form of more taxes than you had planned to pay them.

But even if you do some planning, there is another significant bridge that must be crossed. Anyone would agree that estate planning can be a very disagreeable subject to think about and discuss. It involves *your* death or the death of your spouse, and those who will benefit from it. This can lead to a common ailment, to which we are all subject: procrastination. Procrastination is knowing that you have to do something, in this particular case estate planning, and simply putting it off to another time. It is not the same as not caring whether it ever gets done. It may be a very disagreeable subject, but one that must be addressed.

Estate planning is not a sudden action accomplished in one fell swoop. It is, instead, a **series** of well thought-out actions by which you plan the accumulation, conservation, management, and eventual disposition of your estate so that you and your beneficiaries may obtain the maximum benefit during your lifetime and after your death. It is not merely having a will drafted and then placing it in a safety deposit box and forgetting about it. Many people do this and think they have done what is necessary. Estate planning is, on the contrary, a continuing and ongoing process of reviewing your legal, financial, and family situation. Any changes in your family's status that might affect your estate in any way can require revisions in your plan so that your beneficiaries are adequately protected. The plan must also reflect changes in federal laws and new developments in the form of Internal Revenue Service (IRS) rulings, court decisions, and state and local statutes in addition to estate planning techniques that may have an effect on accumulation or retention of your wealth for you and your beneficiaries.

There are many options to systematically consider in developing a viable estate plan. It may involve establishing an irrevocable trust, a charitable trust, gifting every year, insurance planning, the use of an insurance trust, employing the marital deduction or using the unified credit while you are alive. If you choose not to do any estate or tax planning or not to develop a program of wealth creation, growth, and retention, your later years, that might have been happy and substantially free of financial worry, can end up as a very unpleasant experience. Even a spasmodic plan that will consider the correct utilization of your resources can help. But a plan of action that is visible and orderly, wherein a specified purpose and pattern is set forth, will be appreciated late in life not only by you, your spouse, and entire family, but by others who are dependent on your efforts to protect them financially during changing and perhaps difficult times, as well.

We live in a period in which the government, over the years, has attempted to restrain and reduce our ability to transfer and distribute property to others without payment of substantial transfer taxes. Taxation, without a doubt, has become the greatest impediment to the transfer of wealth between generations. As a result, building an estate is appreciably more difficult now than it has been in former years. With our current tax structure designed to remove whatever loopholes are present (many have already disappeared), your ability to save and benefit yourself and, in addition, provide your family with financial security in your later years and after death has been substantially reduced. Federal and state taxes on income, probate expenses, and settlement and legal costs must be paid, depleting what remains for beneficiaries. Recognizing this, more and more forward-looking individuals such as yourself are seeking ways prior to their death, to **retain** as much wealth as they can. This means that you must invest your money so you can attain a sufficient rate or return to provide your family with income and appreciation of principal. This, indeed, is the other side of estate planning: merging tax planning with a well thought-out estate plan that includes the use of trusts, combined with money management. This will be our focus.

Certainly astute growth of your asset base while you are alive, and postmortem management of this property for the benefit of your spouse and others after you die, can be critical to the success of your overall long-term program. What should your role be in this regard? How can you oversee your assets properly on a current basis and administer an effective investment plan until such time as you have to give up control to someone else because of poor health or death? For instance, should you manage the money yourself and purchase individual shares of common stock, bonds, or a money market instrument or should you perhaps seek investment advice from a professional? Should your money be placed in a trust with a financial institution managing it? These questions are personal and as such depend on each individual's expertise and experience in investing in the securities market. Investment decisions can eventually have a great deal to do with how much you have and how much of your estate goes to beneficiaries. A poorly managed investment portfolio can leave the very ones that you wish to protect in financial jeopardy.

Another point to consider is the amount of income you and/or your spouse, and perhaps other beneficiaries, will need. One can make projections on rates of return, but at best they are educated guesses. No one knows what the inflation rate will be ten years from today and how it will affect you or your spouse's purchasing power and income requirements. Most people, as they get older and retire, will have to face living on social security benefits plus what they receive from a government or private pension. Others may have done some planning and have additional dividends or interest income from investments. Will you be in this group? Will your income be sufficient? We have to assume it may not be based on our past history of rising prices and the persistent loss of purchasing power over the years. Is this a challenge that you can accept?

There is no doubt that reading any book is something like going on a quest, whether you read a novel for the pleasure it gives you as the story unfolds, a mystery for the resolution of a plot, or non-fiction for the purpose of acquiring information that will provide some understanding of an important subject. When you complete this book, you should be able to establish an outline of what the possibilities are for you, and then attempt to piece together your initial estate plan, and outline and establish guidelines for a more formal arrangement later on. This is the essence and the overall purpose of this introduction to estate planning and asset protection.

Before going on to the next chapter, I would like to emphasize that because the laws of dying and transferring wealth are so complex and ever-changing, this should not be considered a Do It Yourself book. Indeed, in my opinion, it would be imprudent to do anything that is legally binding or irrevocable in nature until you feel confident that you possess the background knowledge and have the access to experienced professional advice to help guide you through the kind of estate plan that **you** have decided upon.

2

Taking the First Step

Estate planning is essentially creating, investigating, managing, utilizing, conserving, and eventually making provisions to transfer as much of your residual estate to whomever you choose. An "estate" is made up of property both personal and real and titled in the name of the decedent at the moment of death. All of the assets belonging to the decedent are subsequently distributed to the entitled beneficiaries after the payment of appropriate taxes, expenses, and debts of the estate. The estate is settled under the laws of the state having legal jurisdiction, after it has been established where the decedent was legally domiciled at the time of death.

The planning of your estate should not begin and end with an off-the-shelf, standardized, preprinted set of documents. You may think that you are saving some money by doing it all yourself, but you won't have the confidence that your plan is the best it can be unless you get the help of experts in their respective fields who know much more than you do. It is also a decision-making process of a personal nature that can take both time and effort, in which you are the one who will eventually decide what is going to happen to the assets you own and in what manner you should transfer or dispose of your property. In other words, who will benefit and who will not, and when is the property to be transferred by your beneficiaries. The plan not only deals with your objectives and desires, but also with how they can be put into language that becomes legally binding.

After you have spent some time in deciding what you want to do with the property that you have accumulated in your lifetime, and who shall be your beneficiaries, you might think about seeing an attorney to have a will drafted. Before you do this, however, think your actions through because you are doing something legal and will be held to what the document says. Having a will drawn is not a hasty and precipitous action. Because you awake one morning and find out that your next door neighbor had a heart attack and died doesn't necessarily mean that you should rush off to the first attorney you can think of to have one drafted. On the contrary, it should be done when you have the time to think about it and are in a relaxed state of mind.

While you are considering your objectives, you might ask yourself *what your estate plan should take into account.* For instance, it should

1. address human, spousal, and family concerns, have a balance, a semblance of equity, and sum up your wishes for the future.
2. be a systematic, constructive, and thoughtful process that attempts to carry out your financial objectives for yourself and your beneficiaries.
3. seek ways to reduce conflicts or tensions that may arise in the family among beneficiaries. Early private communication with family members can lead to less strain and some positive results.
4. attempt to increase the value of the assets that are under your control or under someone to whom you have given control.

5. take into account estate tax considerations and employ ways described in this book in which estate tax liability can be substantially reduced or effectively eliminated.
6. require that legal and administrative expenses be kept to a minimum.
7. specify periodic reviews of the plan itself to allow your own changes and adjustments resulting from new laws that could have a bearing on and effect the interests of you and your beneficiaries.
8. be structured so that sufficient liquidity will be available to avoid any forced sale of valuable assets to pay estate tax liability. Life insurance, investment securities that can easily be sold, and bank accounts can meet this requirement.
9. have a selected group of professionals whom you trust and who have your best interest in mind in implementing an appropriate estate plan. It is your responsibility to gather this team together working for your established goals.

The Will

The will is the basic legal instrument in after-death estate transfers. It will serve to pinpoint your intentions and, perhaps with other legal instruments, develop a coherent transfer plan to fit together the jigsaw puzzle of assets and of personal obligations, desires, and promises to the family and to others who are not family members. If you care about who gets your hard-earned savings, securities, property, or whatever else you own when you die, be certain that you have a proper will. What is regrettable is that many people have not provided for the distribution of their assets and, as a result, persons they would have liked to have received a portion of their assets are left out.

There is little question that the execution of a will in written form is critical in planning your estate. It is a declaration of your intent and it directs and provides for the management and disposition of your property. But it has no legal effect and confers no rights prior to your death. The maker of the will must be able to understand the nature of the document and the legal consequences in signing it. This is called *testamentary capacity*. Additionally, when a will is drawn, it should (1) have a plan for distribution of assets, (2) not be under the control of another person, and (3) not have any semblance of fraud involved.

Any will should be witnessed, and in most states at least two witnesses are required. It is necessary that they be adults (over eighteen years of age) with a minimum standard of intelligence and the awareness that a will is being signed. It is also incumbent upon them to understand the nature of the document and relate at some later date what happened during the signing, if necessary. It should also be notarized.

There are many states that will authorize what are sometimes known as *self-proving wills*. A will becomes self-proving when the signatures of the testator and the witnesses are notarized and they sign the instrument in each other's presence. Having a self-proving will can avoid, sometime in the future, the necessity of any witness testifying as to the proper execution of the will at the death of the testator. In addition to signing the document, each page should be initialed.

As an instrument executed with a degree of formality, a will must also serve to clarify any new developments or modifications in the law or in your life and the lives of persons named in the will. It should reflect changes in marital status, births and deaths of family members that may effect the purpose and objectives of you as testator. For example, let's say that, after the will is executed, you marry and a child is either adopted or born during the marriage. If this event is not provided for in the document it may cause revocation in certain states. Revocation of a will can also take place by destroying it through burning, mutilating, cutting or tearing it yourself, or by another person if it is in your presence and you have given permission to do so. It can also be revoked by a subsequent will provided it says so directly or indirectly. Final divorce or annulment may also revoke a will.

What Are the Advantages of Having a Will?

If you die intestate, that is without a will, the state in which you are domiciled will pass property to certain relatives of yours following an order of inheritance. Laws of descent and distribution have been drafted by the states to be "fair" in the average situation to beneficiaries, but most of us would like to choose to whom and under what circumstances we leave our property when we die. A will, properly drafted and executed, will allow you to do this. You will be able to not only choose your beneficiaries but how and when they are to receive the property. In addition, a will can make provisions to revoke any prior wills, forgive any debts that are owed to you, state who you choose to disinherit with the exception of your spouse, and what should be done concerning a minor or disabled child if death occurs to both spouses. Burial instructions involving you and your spouse can also be addressed.

If you choose to, you may also bequeath specific items of furniture, jewelry, heirlooms, or make cash bequests, and be certain that they will pass to the proper persons. Without a will, written or oral instructions may not be followed. But you can make additions or change your will by adding a codicil. This must be executed formally and be subject to the same exactness and scrutiny as the will itself. It must have a date, and must be attested to by witnesses. The real test of legality and effectiveness of a will is its fairness. Many jurisdictions will refuse to enforce a will that attempts to rule money or property away from children or spouse.

Having a will can also authorize the continuation of a business with specific recommendations as to who would take over. If those persons mentioned were not inclined to do so, the executor might have to do it. Many executors, however, are busy on their own and would not elect to accept that responsibility. If the executor agreed, he or she might not want to accept any associated financial risk and would probably want to be compensated handsomely.

With few exceptions, every executor must provide a surety bond to secure an honest and faithful performance of his or her duties. The testator, however, may waive this requirement in the will. If there is no will, the court will require a fiduciary bond to be posted by whoever is named to administer the estate. This adds cost and must be paid for by the estate. Other costs should also be minimized, such as requiring the executor to publish a notice of sale in the newspapers for the disposition of assets to pay probate costs and death taxes.

Pour-Over Will

A "pour-over" provision in a will is created by you before or at the time the will is signed and is usually employed in conjunction with an existing revocable trust (discussed later). It insures that any assets titled in your name at the time of death and remaining in your name either inadvertently or otherwise, will pass to a trust and be distributed to beneficiaries or managed in accordance with the terms included in the trust document. The transfer of these assets occurs after probate takes place and after expenses, debts, and taxes have been paid.

Contesting a Will

When a will is contested, its validity is challenged in the court for the purpose of having its provisions set aside. It can take place when it appears that (1) undue influence played a part when the will was written, (2) the will did not adhere to the laws or fulfill the statutory requirements of the jurisdiction or state in which it was drawn, (3) there was fraud involved, (4) the person making the will was not sufficiently competent at the time to understand what he or she was doing, (5) the person was not of legal age or (6) possible forgery was involved. Very often wills are contested by dissatisfied and angry relatives after deciding that they have not received their just share of the decedent's properties. As a matter of fact, a friend or relative or anyone else, for that matter, left out of a will should do nothing for a period of time. If he or she continues to feel anger and there are solid grounds to contest the will, then legal action may be taken. Contestation cases, however, are not easy to validate because there is a presumption in estate law that a will ruled legal by the court reflects the last wishes and desires of the testator. One would have to challenge this presumption. In addition, if the challenger chose to pursue the contest, it would be very costly and could very well take two or three years, perhaps even longer, before it was resolved.

Everything mentioned so far suggests that a great deal of care must be taken in drafting, executing, and signing a will. A will contest cannot be ignored, but the chances of it occurring can be lessened by having an anticontest provision placed in the will. Such a provision simply states that anyone who contests the will forfeits any bequest made to that person under the terms of the will. Placing all of your assets under the umbrella of a trust instrument will prevent the possibility of a will contest that can be disruptive and lead to nasty consequences for members of the family and perhaps close friends.

As was said, if you die intestate, your estate will be distributed in accordance with the laws of the state in which you are domiciled. Such laws have no flexibility and make little or no allowance for the needs of particular beneficiaries. Generally, the surviving spouse and the children will be first to share in the estate. After that, come the blood descendants of the deceased, his or her parents, and, lastly, those persons not descendants but related to the deceased through a common ancestor.

Probate

Probate is a process whereby the last will and testament of the deceased person is declared valid or not. It is a legal mechanism through which the law deals with settling an estate and a procedure that clears title to your property so that ownership can be transferred from one person to another. This is done under the direction and approval of the probate court, providing that the will becomes effective and the court has jurisdiction and accepts the will as a legal and valid instrument. This procedure by the court leading to the acceptance of the will that expresses the final wishes of the decedent is called the probate process. Nothing can happen, however, until the will is on record with the probate court. The executor must then petition the court to approve the will. If the executor does not do this, then another interested party may.

If there are no delays, the probate process will usually take about a year to complete and can lead to frustrations for the spouse and beneficiaries. Another irritation to some may be that the filing becomes a matter of public record. Everyone can know your private business. Your will, the beneficiaries named, and those that were disinherited, all are in the record and available to anyone who wishes to know. Copies can be made easily, and the entire proceeding can be reviewed at any time.

Ownership Forms Not Subject to Probate

Because of the lack of privacy, delays, red tape, and inevitable costs involved, you should determine beforehand what assets, if any, you would like to pass to beneficiaries under your will and which can successfully avoid the probate process. Generally speaking, probate can be avoided by employing the following ownership forms.

Property passing by operation of law includes certain forms of joint ownerships, including *Tenancy by the entirety*. This is a form of joint-ownership that exists between the husband and a wife in which property can freely pass to the surviving spouse upon the death of the first spouse without any tax liability. It can only be terminated when death or divorce occurs or by the consent of both parties, and it is *not* subject to probate.

Under *joint tenancy with rights of survivorship*, property also passes automatically to the survivor and the agreement can be terminated unilaterally. Furthermore, this form of ownership is not effected or influenced by the terms of the will or controlled by any conditions stated in a trust document. It also is *not* subject to the probate process.

Other forms of property that are not subject to probate and that pass under a valid and legal contract are *insurance* proceeds, *pension and profit sharing plan assets*, and proceeds from an *annuity*. In addition, a *trust arrangement*, in which one or more parties holds or manages property for the benefit of another, can also avoid probate or at least minimize the need for probate. It should be understood that the alternatives mentioned here are not substitutes for a will but are employed in conjunction with a will.

Tenancy in common is a slightly different arrangement in which property does not pass by operation of law. Although each tenant has an "undivided interest" and is entitled to a proportionate share in investment income, for instance, there is no right of survivorship. Each owner may transfer, sell, gift, encumber, bequeath, or dispose of his or her interest by any means. The property *is* subject to probate.

Many people are under the impression that avoiding probate will reduce or even completely eliminate one's tax liability. This is just not true. It is quite possible to have all your property titled in such a way as to avoid probate, but you are still going to have to pay any estate tax that may be assessed. The principles in the law that govern probate and tax liability are completely different. Probate is largely a legal process in which the estate pays fees and expenses to pass property from the decedent to heirs and beneficiaries. Estate taxes, by comparison, are based on ownership and control of property and have little to do with whether the property is a probated or a nonprobated item. The concept is manifested very simply when joint property is concerned. For example, a father buys a boat and places title in joint ownership with his son. When the father dies the boat will pass to the son as a nonprobatable item. Will it avoid going through the father's estate at death? Not likely. Will it be subject to estate tax? Probably so!

Choosing an Executor

One of the decisions you will have to make sooner or later is who will be your executor, sometimes known as a personal representative. It would behoove you to choose someone who is an experienced and knowledgeable person, rather than just someone you know or who is a friend of the family. The person must exercise due diligence in disbursing payments to beneficiaries, in making investment decisions if given the power to do so, and in avoiding unnecessary expenses. In addition, the executor(rix) should hire the right professionals to help settle the estate and basically handle its disposition in a businesslike manner so there are no delays because of management inefficiencies. The point here is that the person you name will have control over your assets for a period of time and will have to deal with your spouse and other beneficiaries. With a will, you have a direct say as to who this person is. If you have no will, the judge will look at the possible candidates to administer the estate and may select one that you would have not chosen. So, you can have the peace of mind of making your choice through naming that person in the will.

What are the duties of the executor? The executor named in the will

1. requests and receives a federal identification number for the estate issued by the IRS;
2. notifies the IRS as to the name of the personal representative (executor) acting for the estate;
3. collects the income in the form of rent receipts from real estate, dividends from common stock, interest

on bank accounts, corporate or tax free bonds, and
from other assets owned by the estate.

4. is obligated to protect property, both personal and
real against harm or loss, for later distribution to the
beneficiaries;

5. follows up on any claims against other people that
the decedent or the estate may have;

6. pays valid expenses and any debts that are owed by
the decedent;

7. makes an inventory of all properties and places appropriate verified appraisals on each;

8. after determining what properties (or income) are
subject to tax, prepares income and estate tax returns with the help of professionals;

9. liquidates assets, if necessary, and distributes personal effects of the testator among relatives and
others.

The duties of the executor end when all the beneficiaries are accounted for and all properties are distributed
in accordance with the law and the will. If the will does
not name an executor, or if the executor named does not
wish to serve and there is no successor-executor capable
of serving and able and willing to be appointed, in most
cases the surviving spouse will have the first right to be
appointed. The surviving spouse may, however, choose
not to serve. If there is no surviving spouse, then the children have the right to be appointed. But are these people
responsible? Do they have the desire and the expertise to
protect the assets of the estate? Is there bitterness among
the children or petty jealousies or other disharmonies
that are likely to have a negative effect on the administration of the estate? Certainly, any of these elements can
lead to higher than normal costs at best, and mismanagement and possible depletion of assets at worst. In addition, the one that agrees to administer the estate has to

have the ability to perform in an atmosphere of increasing governmental regulation, red tape, and tax complexity.

Durable Power of Attorney

If you are unable to make important decisions because of poor health or incapacity, the use of a durable power of attorney can be as pivotal to you and your family as the drafting of a will was important (or a trust discussed in a later chapter may be) in the development of your estate plan. As we get older, we become less able to perform certain everyday functions that were easy earlier but now seem overly complex. Making an investment decision or paying your monthly electric bill can become burdensome. Indeed, even a temporary medical condition can leave you unable to function as you ordinarily would for an extended period of time. With the possibility of something like this occurring, a prudent and forward-looking planner would be wise to prepare for that unfortunate time. You may become seriously ill, incapacitated, mentally incompetent, or just have your health deteriorate to the point where someone else whom you designate has to completely take over for you. If you do nothing, and one of several occurrences just mentioned takes place, the court will be required to appoint someone to act and make decisions in your place.

In order to avoid this, you should draft two separate *durable powers of attorney*— one for health care and another for financial matters—allowing you to name an agent(s) who will have the authority to act for you in the event you are unable to act for yourself. The clause generally included with a power of attorney is referred to as the "durable power clause." It states, in effect, that the power will remain in force even if you become incapacitated or mentally incompetent. It merely appoints another person or persons to make health care decisions and financial decisions for you because of either physical or mental limitations. The person(s) that is named becomes the "attorney in fact" and has access to all medical records and makes the medical decisions subject to any limitations stated in the power when it was drafted and signed.

Because medical technology has advanced so much in the last decade, terminally ill persons can be kept alive for an extended period of time. If you would like a natural death, not being dependent on wires and tubes, preferring to leave this world with a modicum of dignity, then you can choose to prohibit the use of life support systems to prolong your life. You will, however, have to state your preferences clearly as to what you would like done so those empowered to do so can carry out your wishes.

The durable powers of attorney are more broadly based than the much advertised and discussed "living will." The authority of the living will is limited to those situations in which the patient is terminally ill and nearing death. The "durable powers," on the other hand, allow specific health care and financial decisions to be made by those having the power, based on current and past medical records, knowledge of the condition, and other information as to what the patient would like to have accomplished. It becomes effective immediately after it is granted, but the patient can continue to make decisions until the power is needed. You can revoke or change any power of attorney as you wish if you are competent to do so.

Advance Medical Directive

Although the durable power of attorney for health care remains a consistently accepted instrument in most jurisdictions to effectively communicate medical choices and preferences regarding health care decisions, additional protection has been promoted recently by a few states by passing new legislation in which the requirement for specific language would be even more precise in letting your wishes be known. For instance, the state of Maryland passed what is known as the Health Care Decision Act that became effective for its residents October 1, 1993. The act sets forth the authority for you and your physician(s), by use of an Advance Medical Directive that is prepared and signed, to allow your appointed "agent" to make health care decisions regarding your consent to, and withholding of, medical treatment, among other things. If no agent is appointed then, at least in the state of Maryland, the act provides for the designation of a surrogate decision maker from a list of relatives. If a relative is not available, then a close friend may be appointed.

The advance directive can afford you some additional protection because it attempts to better clarify the effectiveness of your medical instructions that may be somewhat unclear in other prepared documents. The directive also represents a significant step in simplifying the whole area of the medical decision-making process.

Conservatorship

If you do not currently have a durable power of attorney for your financial affairs and you become incapacitated, physically impaired, senile, or incompetent and unable to administer your property, then in the absence of any other legal instrument properly executed, the court will do what it must and appoint another person or entity to protect your assets. This, however, need not occur if you have made provisions prior to a catastrophic event for the investment management and financial administration of your assets through a living trust, pour-over will, or codicil to a will. Here, someone given authority to act in your behalf will provide oversight administrative functions.

What can take place if you have not prepared a legal instrument to protect your assets is that concerned relatives will file papers with the court to see that someone be appointed as conservator. They may provide the court with the names of certain nominees and one of several may be chosen. But the judge will consider many factors in appointing a "guardian of your property." The selection will be based on many factors but mainly on who will serve your best interests and those of the immediate family. The one chosen by the judge may not have been your nominee if you had properly planned ahead.

Indeed, having a court appointed conservator can be expensive. There are legal fees, papers to file and the time consumed in dealing with lawyers and courts. Disagreements can also erupt between family members and perhaps interference by one who wishes to change the investment strategy or financial administration of your investment assets.

Minor children, especially those that will be the eventual owners of a large inheritance, also need supervision and management of the property that they will inherit because minors cannot legally transfer titled property. If a minor inherits, for instance, a retirement account or some shares of stock or is to receive the proceeds from an insurance policy, the court may have to sign for the child in the absence of any legal document or provisions to the contrary. If you have already established a trust, the assets, in all probability, have been placed into the trust and no eventual probate costs are involved. If, however, a will is used, the probate process will have to take place for the will to be validated. This, as we have learned, can, in some instances, take over a year. It should also be noted that each child's share of any possible estate must be held in a conservatorship account until the child attains the age of eighteen (or twenty-one) at which time the entire remaining share is distributed outright.

When a court-appointed conservator is required, the court will see to it that an inventory of property will be first filed and reports submitted to it showing receipts and disbursements for the period. At your death, a final report is prepared and submitted to the court, which then discharges the conservator and turns over the remaining assets to the decedent's personal representative, also known as the executor or the executrix and used interchangeably here.

Although you may have prepared a will or a trust and you have named an executor or successor trustee, if the documents were not signed, witnessed and/or notarized properly and you suffer a stroke or heart attack, the documents will have no force and effect.

Guardianship

One of the more important decisions that you will have to make in planning your total estate package is to make certain that there is someone to take care of you if and when you become sick, are declared incompetent, disabled, or otherwise physically or emotionally unable to perform your everyday needs. Although precisely not the same procedure, it is similar to choosing an executor or a successor trustee. Appointing a guardian to take care of your personal and health care needs or those of an aging parent, grandparent, or minor child is pivotal if you are to have a complete estate plan. You will have to choose the one you want, and that person must accept your offer or reject it. Of course, your designee can always change his or her mind later on.

When you attempt to identify a possible candidate, a relative may or may not be the most appropriate prospect, but because of family ties they are the first to come to mind. Serious consideration, however, must be given to the financial condition of the potential appointee as well as to his or her health, age, ability and willingness to care for your children over a period of years. If you have found such a person then provisions in a will or a living trust instrument or other legal alternative can be planned and executed so as to prevent the appointment of a guardian through a formal process, usually by the probate court.

Basically, guardianship takes place when an individual is appointed by the court and given authority to make decisions for another. It can be a necessary step when certain events take place requiring the court to intervene. The specific powers granted to a court-appointed guardian can vary from state to state, but generally are limited to meet the requirements of the individuals concerned. More specifically, minor children whose interests need to be protected on a personal level with education, training, a proper home, and a loving atmosphere.

For instance, you have teenage children whom you wish to protect in case a catastrophic event takes place. If you have a living trust, the successor trustee will be obligated to make provisions for them when you cannot. This doesn't mean that the court will not get involved; it only means they are less likely, and only so when they may be pressed by other members of the family. Certainly, if provisions have not been worked out before a triggering event occurs, and there is no proper legal instrument to tell the court what to do or at least what your wishes are, the court will be obliged to appoint a guardian of its own for your minor children until they reach maturity. Therefore, see to it that you have an "appointment of guardian provision," which is made part of a living trust instrument. This can be done after you have chosen the person whom you respect, and who has the same values as you and your spouse, to protect your loved ones.

Estate Settlement Costs

Shortly after the death of an individual, the costs of settling the estate become due and payable with available funds. For example, a surety bond will have to be furnished in many states to protect the beneficiaries and creditors of the estate. The minimum charges for such a bond must be borne from monies that are currently accessible in the estate and made available to the executor. Because of this requirement, and others, the estate planner should look ahead to determine how such expenses will be paid and to find ways to prevent excessive estate shrinkage by reducing frivolous and unnecessary settlement payments as much as possible.

What are the costs of settling an estate? They include medical costs and other expenses related to the decedent's last illness, debts of the decedent, funeral and burial expenses, probate expenses, executor and administration fees, appraiser's fees, court costs, attorney's fees and, of course, federal estate taxes, and inheritance taxes. Estate tax rates range from a graduated scale from 18 to 55 percent, starting at a base of $600,000 of a taxable estate.* But there are provisions in the law that permit deductions for debts and administration costs incurred by the decedent's estate and reduce tax liability. State death taxes vary. Fees paid to the estate planning attorney, the executor, and others in the settlement process are examined by the court to determine whether or not the charges

---

*See estate tax rate chart in Chapter 3.

were fair. Settlement costs can be high if the estate is complicated and requires a great deal of time. Probate fees in and of themselves can run between 5–9 percent of the gross estate.

Minimizing Legal Fees and Expenses

You can try to reduce legal fees related to planning your estate by having as few strings as possible. If your estate is in order and not very complicated, the fees should be modest. Know generally what you need and want in an estate plan by doing the basic research before spending money on a lot of professional fees. This is one of the purposes of this book. But, after this background is accomplished, your estate has to be set up properly, and it is your responsibility to choose the right professionals to work with you.

After you die, there can be a lot of work in legally disposing of your estate, and the one you name as executor will have the most to do. The executor or personal representative can be your lawyer, but need not be. It would be a person you nominate when you write your will to carry out your directions and requests as stated in the document. The executor will have to clear up the maze of paperwork, including affidavits, appraisals of real and personal property, quotations on common stocks and other securities, etc. In addition, the executor, administrator, or legal representative of the taxpayer who dies during the year must file a federal income tax return for the decedent generally due the fifteenth day of the fourth month after the close of the decedent's normal tax year. When filing a copy of the death certificate must be included with the proper forms. Estate planning expenses that are incurred related to investment and income tax planning are deductible as miscellaneous expenses in the year in which they are incurred, but only if they exceed 2 percent of adjusted gross income (AGI). Fees paid for the preparation of a will, including the "pour-over" type, cannot be included in the deduction.

Preliminary Steps for Survivors

So far in this chapter the focus has been on the estate planner. But what of the survivor(s)? *What can they do to expedite the work done by the executor?* From their standpoint, after the death of the spouse, a series of events usually take place. Below is a typical chronology and a set of preliminary steps that can be an aid to you as a surviving spouse and other survivors in helping settle the estate.

1. Locate will and trust documents
2. Make funeral arrangements
3. Confer with an attorney and meet with trust administrators and others in the estate planning team
4. Talk with beneficiaries
5. Safeguard assets
6. Protect property
7. Check insurance
8. Notify banks and check on trust arrangements
9. Examine decedent's books and records
10. Begin probate of will
11. Assemble and make inventory of assets
12. Collect debts
13. Appraise assets
14. Analyze business interests (supervise, sell, or liquidate)
15. Retain or sell securities based on market conditions
16. Manage or sell real estate

17. Decide on the disposition of house and household effects
18. Determine any claims against estate
19. Pay taxes
20. Final distribution to all

As we have discussed, a will is an integral part of an estate plan and is designed to dispose and distribute your property at death in a manner in which you see fit. If you choose not to have a will, or no will can be found, then the state laws of intestacy, descent and distribution will divide your estate accordingly. If such a distribution of your assets is how you wish it to be handled, then when you die the state will do what it has to. If, however, you care about your spouse and family, you will make every effort to see that they receive as much of your estate as is legally possible.

Unfortunately, many people never get around to having a will prepared. They either lack the motivation, cannot confront their own mortality, or procrastinate until it is too late. There are others who are under the supposition that, if all their property is jointly held, they don't need a will. If you want to have control over who receives your assets, you might try sitting down one night to decide who the people are and under what circumstances you would like them to benefit in your will. Remember, a will can be written, but, if it is not properly executed, it may serve no purpose. Think of it as something you are doing not only for yourself in winding up your affairs, but in constructively providing a mechanism for the transfer of assets to those whom you choose.

3

Estate, Gift, and Inheritance Taxes

One of the most misunderstood concepts in estate planning is the notion that, if one can in some way remove certain assets or, as a matter of fact, all of one's property from the probate process, then that person is going to save estate taxes. Unfortunately, this is not the case. Probate is concerned with the passing of property legally to others. Estate taxes are based on ownership and control of property *whether or not* it is probatable. An example of this has to do with taxation of joint property discussed in the preceding chapter. We learned that certain forms of joint ownership of property pass to the survivor by operation of law and there is no probate required. But the *value* of the property, or a part thereof, is included in the decedent's estate and can be subject to estate taxes if he or she owns the property at death. The federal government, in addition, will levy a gift tax on the value above a certain level of property transfers made during your lifetime.

Tax rates for transfers are illustrated in table 3.1. Any citizen is currently permitted to give away up to $600,000 free of estate tax liability during his or her lifetime or at death. In addition, gifts of up to $10,000 per donee may be made each year tax-free by the donor. Estate tax is applied against the value of the decedent's estate, and the tax rate and eventual liability, if any, is determined by its size. A lifetime credit of $192,800 is available to all citizens to offset those taxes. To give a very simple example of how taxable amounts are determined, let us say that Mr. Jones dies and leaves a taxable estate valued at $1,000,000. By examining the tax rate shown in table 3.1 you will find that the tax on that amount is $345,800. Mr. Jones, however, can use the unified credit of $192,800, to reduce his net tax—$345,800 minus $192,800, which becomes a $153,000 tax liability. Any state taxes that may be required to be paid are not included here.

Estimating Your Estate Tax

Calculation of your federal estate tax liability generally begins with the total value of the property in your estate. This is referred to as your gross estate and is the cumulative fair market value of all assets titled in your name. The specific amount can be established on one of two dates: the date of death or six months after the date of death. The state in which you are domiciled, that is, where you legally reside, will on that date generally determine from where your tax return should be filed (IRS filing form #706).

Estate tax is a tax on your wealth. It is assessed, for example, against such property as investment securities, proceeds from life insurance from a policy owned or controlled by you, any ownership held in joint names, bank accounts including "payable on death" (POD) accounts (sometimes known as "in trust for" accounts), coin and stamp collections, art works, personal effects, property and property rights, annuities that pass through to beneficiaries, property held in a revocable trust account that was created by you and can be revoked by you, pension and profit sharing plans and retirement accounts. Outstanding mortgages or other liens you may have are excluded from the computation.

For example, let us say you have added up both your real and personal property and find your gross estate is valued at $1,200,000. Your next step is to subtract those items permitted by law to reduce your gross estate, such as an existing mortgage on your home. This will give you your net estate which can be further reduced by property given to your spouse under the unlimited marital deduction. This figure is your *net taxable estate* and, if it is not greater than the $600,000 threshold—the lifetime exemption equivalent, then you would not be subject to any estate tax.

A very simple statement is shown in figure 3.1.

Employing the Tax Credit*

The tax liability that your estate would be responsible for on a $600,000 net taxable amount under current law would be $192,800. Since 1987, the unified gift tax credit has been established as $192,800 and is equivalent to a taxable estate of $600,000. So the credit you receive offsets the liability of your net taxable estate of $600,000, and you owe nothing. Everyone—married, single, adult, child—receives this exemption. The credit of $192,800 as applied can be the most important objective in planning the transfer of assets out of your estate, and it can exempt a substantial amount of your wealth from tax liability. Portions of the credit may be drawn upon as

---

*It is possible that the lifetime exemption equivalent will be modified sometime in the future. Currently, Congress is discussing a possible increase in the exemption. The question of indexing these amounts and that of the annual exclusion has also been debated. Check with your financial adviser on any last minute changes.

TABLE 3.1
Unified Estate and Gift Tax Rates on Taxable Estates

(A) Amount subject to tax		Tax on amount in Column A	Tax Rate on excess over amount in Column A Percent
exceeding	but not exceeding		
$ 0	$ 10,000	$ 0	18
10,000	20,000	1,800	20
20,000	40,000	3,800	22
40,000	60,000	8,200	24
60,000	80,000	13,000	26
80,000	100,000	18,200	28
100,000	150,000	23,800	30
150,000	250,000	38,800	32
250,000	500,000	70,800	34
500,000	750,000	155,800	37
750,000	1,000,000	248,300	39
1,000,000	1,250,000	345,800	41
1,250,000	1,500,000	448,300	43
1,500,000	2,000,000	555,800	45
2,000,000	2,500,000	780,800	49
2,500,000	3,000,000	1,025,800	53
3,000,000	10,000,000	1,290,800	55
10,000,000		5,140,800	60
21,040,000		11,764,800	55
21,040,000			

needed until used up. This can be done while you are alive but you can still maintain the exemption at death.

The Annual Exclusion

Under current law, gift tax is required to be paid when there is transfer of funds in excess of $10,000 in any one calendar year to any one person. The donor is permitted this annual exclusion per donee each year providing it as a gift of "present interest." This means that the donee

Gross Estate		1,200,000
Mortgage on personal home	$160,000	
Mortgage on acreage	40,000	
Mortgage total	$200,000	200,000
Gross estate minus mortgages		1,000,000

Subtract Expenses

Funeral Cost	$ 10,000	
Probate and administrative costs	40,000	
Last illness expense	20,000	
Credit card liability	5,000	
Other personal debts	5,000	
Charitable gifts	20,000	
Total Expenses	$100,000 (minus)	− 100,000
Total Net Estate		900,000
Inheritance to spouse under marital deduction (minus)		− 300,000
Net Taxable Estate:		$600,000

(Amount above this exemption limit would be taxable)

Figure 3.1 Computing Your Net Taxable Estate

must have an "unrestricted right to the immediate use, possession and enjoyment" of the property. If the property can only be used in the future it will in all probability result in a taxable event. Employing the annual exclusion is pivotal in reducing the size of your taxable estate. If, however, you don't use it in any one year it will be lost forever.

Additionally, if you are planning to make a one-time gift currently, or systematically, such as every year to members of the family to lessen your eventual estate tax liability when you die, don't wait until the last day of the year to complete the gift. Such a gift could include shares of stock and other financial assets or certificates registered in your name. The effective date of the gift however, is not the date on which you give the certificate to the donee but instead the date upon which ownership is, in fact, transferred on the books of the brokerage firm, bank, or trust company.

This is also true of shares held in "street name" at a brokerage firm. Changing ownership into someone else's name can take as much as four to five weeks after orders are issued. It would behoove you to begin the process at least two or three months before you wish the change to be a legal transfer. If this is not done properly, what was supposed to be two nontaxable transfers of $10,000 a year, perhaps one in December and one in January of the following year, can become two transfers in one year, creating tax liability on one of the gifts. When you give shares of stock as a gift, certain other rules should be followed: Your records must show the market value of the shares at the time you made the gift. Keep a newspaper indicating the date and the closing price of the shares for verification purposes. In addition, you must have records showing the date of purchase and the price you paid for the shares (the cost basis). The confirmation issued by the brokerage firm will give you that information. In the case of shares of stock or other securities or capital assets that are received as gifts and at some later date sold at a profit, the recipient's cost basis is the same as your basis and he or she is responsible for paying federal capital gains tax when the shares are sold if there is a gain.

Timing a gift can also be of some importance. From an estate planning perspective, and employing tax reduction strategies, consideration should always be given to the tax implications of gifting *highly appreciated* assets while you are still alive. These can be a significant tax benefit to the beneficiary of the property if it is transferred *after* your death and not before. This is so because the law allows the donee to receive the property on a step-up basis. This means that the appreciated asset(s) will escape capital gains liability because its value is based not on what the original cost was, but on its fair market value at the time of death.

Gift Splitting

If you and your spouse make a gift to a third party, the gift can be considered as made one-half by you and one-half by your spouse. This is known as gift splitting. If the gift is $20,000 both of your *must* agree to split the gift and, if you do, you can each take the $10,000 annual exclusion for your part of the gift. As a more striking example, Harold and his wife Helen agree to use gift splitting so that each may give away more than $10,000 without creating a taxable event. Harold gives his nephew George $17,000, and Helen gives her niece Josephine $12,000. Although each gift is larger than the annual exclusion limit of $10,000 per donee, they can, by gift splitting, make these gifts without tax.

The gift Harold made to George is treated as split in two. Half ($8,500) would be from Harold and the other half ($8,500) a gift from Helen. Helen's gift to Josephine is also treated as split in two, half ($6,000) from Helen and half ($6,000) from Harold. In each case, for gift tax purposes, one-half of the split gift is not more than the $10,000 annual exclusion and is not considered to be a taxable gift.

This type of gifting to third parties takes a little more time, effort, and preparation on your part if you wish to take advantage of the gift-splitting concept. There are specific requirements that must be met for you and your spouse to qualify for this type of gift. Among other things, your spouse and you must not only file individual gift tax returns at the same time, but are also required to complete the proper form consenting to the gift as made by each of you. If you and your spouse are willing to conform to these and other specific requirements, you might write or call the IRS and request form #709 and #709A including an instruction booklet. If you don't care to do the paper work yourself, call your accountant or financial adviser. Gift splitting is certainly a worthwhile device—an attractive way to increase the amount of gifting you may make over and above the annual exemption limit and still not pay taxes.

Equalizing Your Estate

Reducing estate taxes through equalization requires the husband and wife working together in a concerted effort toward this purpose. Estate tax equalization is not based on transferring funds from one spouse to another by use of the unlimited marital deduction. On the contrary, such a transfer may shift the entire tax burden to the survivor. Equalization can, on the other hand, require gifting between spouses and may make it necessary to have property owned separately by each spouse. The purpose of all this is to pay a small tax on the death of the first spouse and pay another small tax on the death of the survivor. The two taxes, in many cases, can be less than the tax assessed on the combined estates after the death of the second spouse. The numbers and possible savings have to be worked through with a tax expert using several equalization options in which computations would be based on use of the estate tax tables to determine whether or not it is desirable, or even tax effective, for your particular circumstance. In any case, this concept, as a possible tax saving option, is further elaborated on when employed with an A-B trust arrangement as discussed in chapter 5.

Charitable Giving

Another way to reduce the size of your taxable estate is by making sizable tax-deductible gifts to a charity of your liking. Gifts to charities can be created in your will or be established under a living trust that becomes effective at your death. They must, however, be made to organizations that have received IRS approval and are qualified for you to receive the tax deduction. You can give cash, gifts of appreciated real property, tangible personal property such as shares of stock or other securities, or perhaps a remainder interest in a residence or farm. Or, if you wish, you may just make a *bequest* designating a portion of your assets to be used for the benefit and support of a charitable organization of your choice. To qualify for a tax-deduction for federal tax purposes, you may use a charitable remainder trust or perhaps a pooled income fund not only to escape a long-term capital gains liability on highly appreciated assets but also to receive income from the trust for a period of years or over the beneficiaries' lifetimes. Charitable trusts are discussed in chapter 7.

Gifts to Minors

Gifts that are made to minor children or grandchildren under the Uniform Gift to Minors Act (UGMA) will qualify for the $10,000 per year per donee annual exclusion ($20,000 per married couple). If checks are made to minors at the end of the year, such as Christmas time, make certain that the donee deposits the money promptly to avoid any question as to whether or not it is a gift for the current year. The annual exclusion is a valuable tool and you would not wish to lose it over a technicality. It should also be noted that under current law, all investment income in excess of $1,300 per year to children under fourteen years of age from a gift to minors account, is taxed to the child at the parent's tax rate.

Using Life Insurance

You can also keep money out of your taxable estate by having life insurance, but not as the owner of the policy. By gifting up to $10,000 per year to a donee, perhaps to one or several of your children, and having them use this money to pay yearly premiums on an insurance policy, you are the insured and they are the owners. When you die, the proceeds from the policy go directly to the owners (or other beneficiaries). If you kept ownership yourself without naming a beneficiary, the proceeds would be paid to your estate and be subject to estate tax. Because this type of gift allows the donee to use the money immediately upon receipt, it is a gift of present interest. Additionally, if it is under $10,000, the gift tax exclusion would apply and no gift tax return need be filed. If it is more, then a tax must be paid on the amount over $10,000 *or* that amount can be taken against your lifetime exemption equivalent, which will be reduced. More will be said about this in the chapter on insurance.

Making a Gift By Disclaimer

An efficient strategy for some planners to pass assets to family members or others is by means of a disclaimer. If you are the donee you can't be forced to accept a gift, and by refusing it your interest can pass to someone else. Why would you not accept the gift? Because someone in your family could profit more from receiving it. It is another way for the donor to make a gift to someone of less means and not pay taxes. This gifting method is especially convenient if you were planning to leave a bequest to that person anyway, but it must be done voluntarily and without monetary or other considerations. The property in question can then be forfeited or "disclaimed" by the donee. In the eyes of the law the donee is legally dead and the property automatically passes on to the alternate beneficiary named in the will. In addition, the gift can never be included in the first beneficiary's estate when he or she dies.

For example, let us say that a father leaves a $300,000 estate to a son who has his own estate valued at $700,000. Because the father's estate falls below the current $600,000 lifetime exemption threshold, there is no tax liability for him. When the son dies, however, (assuming no increase in value) the son's estate valuation, having accepted the gift, would be a combined total of $1,000,000. If he had disclaimed the inheritance and allowed it to pass, to a family member in the next generation perhaps, his tax would be assessed only against the $100,000—the difference between the $600,000 exemption and his own $700,000 estate—rather than the $400,000 difference between the exemption and the total of his own and his father's estates.

Indeed, giving up part of an inheritance may be an attractive estate planning tool for the donee, but it also can be advantageous for the donor in intergenerational tax planning. But keep in mind that disclaimers are subject to rules and regulations that can restrict their use. More specifically, a qualified disclaimer must be an unqualified and irrevocable refusal by a person to accept an interest in the property, satisfy the applicable federal and state laws, be in writing, be completed within a month of the gift, require that the person named on that disclaimer has not accepted any benefit from or interest in the prop-

erty, and further require that the property interest passing to the person other than the disclaimant do so
without any direction by the disclaimant.

Gifting Too Much

Before making gifts to anyone, especially your children,
it might be wise to make your most accurate guess—
based on family longevity, mortality tables, and your current health—of how the gift and loss of income that
follows will effect your life currently and in the future
before your own death. Estimate, as best you can, the
level of support you need to sustain your living requirements. You should allow for the loss of purchasing power
because of inflation. Also, consider large items such as
medical and long-term care, insurance, and a reserve for
emergencies as a precondition to gifting. So the basic
question becomes how much of your estate can you give
away and not jeopardize your financial independence
and level of comfort? This is a personal decision as to
what you have and what you will need in the future. Any
economic change or reversal of fortune should be in your
formula. You certainly don't want to become a dependent
person because you have given away too much to donees
who probably will not remember your gratitude anyhow.
   After making these projections as to what and how
much you will require to satisfy your financial needs and
that of your spouse, let us say that you might like to gift
a family summer home to a close relative. You have had
this property for years and it has increased in value. If
you sold it, a large capital gains tax would have to be
paid. You conclude that this gift is warranted and would
be welcomed by other members of the family. And, in
addition, the gift will remove a highly appreciated asset
from your estate for death tax purposes. Why is this so?

Because, as was stated earlier, the cost basis of the property received by the donee is the appraised "fair market value" on the date the gift was made and doesn't subject the donee to any hidden tax liability. Clearly then, making this type of gift or other lifetime gifts, especially if the program continues over a number of years, can be significant in reducing or eliminating the portion of your estate that will be subject to taxes. Be careful, however, not to make gifts in excess of the annual exclusion of $10,000 per year per donee. If you do, you will have to file a gift tax return, which may mean appraisal fees to determine its market value if it is an asset other than money. Additionally, although making gifts can be advisable, even necessary perhaps, from an estate tax perspective other considerations can be important. Might a gift have possible negative influences upon its recipient? Would the money be used appropriately? Certainly it would be unwise to make a substantial irrevocable gift to one that does not have the maturity or the common sense to manage a substantial amount of money.

Filing a Gift Tax Return

Generally, you must file a gift tax return if

1. You gave more than $10,000 during the year to any one person, or
2. you and your spouse are splitting a gift, or
3. you gave someone a gift that he or she cannot actually possess, enjoy, or receive income from until some time in the future, or
4. your spouse's ownership interest in a gift you gave will be ended by some future event.

You do not have to file a return to report gifts to and for the use of political organizations, gifts to charitable organizations, and gifts that are used to pay tuition or medical expenses.

Inheritance Tax

Inheritance tax is assessed on the privilege of *receiving* property from the decedent at death as contrasted with the tax on estates which must be paid to the federal government when property is transferred to another at death. It is not assessed on the property itself but on the right to acquire it by testamentary gift or by descent. The rate of assessment is graded by class according to the relationship of the testator to the particular beneficiary. The lowest level of inheritance tax is imposed on the spouse, lineal decedents, and ancestors. It is then graded up for brothers and sisters with the heaviest tax impositions on uncles, aunts, cousins, and others. Personal exemptions are also permitted in many states but vary from state to state and are also graded by class.

Some states impose inheritance taxes. Others do not. There is also a difference in assessment rates and levels. Your attorney or tax adviser will have to find out how it might effect your personal estate planning. In any case, your executor will, in all probability, be writing two checks for death taxes instead of one. One will go to the federal government for estate taxes and one, to the state in which you are domiciled for inheritance taxes. Although there may be some small tax advantage to be a permanent resident of a state with favorable inheritance tax laws, the likelihood of more than marginal savings would not make it worthwhile for you to effect a change of domicile. When the inheritance tax is paid by the executor to any state for property included in the decedent's gross estate, a credit for that amount is allowed against federal estate tax liability. Also, there are some states that impose a *state* estate tax on a percentage of the value of the net estate. No state, however, imposes both an inheritance tax *and* estate tax.

Marital Deduction

So far, the basic federal tax that estates are responsible for has been described and, in addition, mention has been made of inheritance taxes, state estate taxes, and gifting as a way to reduce tax liability. If you are married, there is another way to reduce or even eliminate estate taxes at your death—through the use of the unlimited marital deduction. To make sure that you qualify for this deduction, the property must be given to the spouse outright.

When the lifetime marital deduction is employed, it allows you to gift, will, or transfer any amount of cash or other property at once or over a period of years to your spouse free of tax liability and without filing any gift tax returns. The device is permitted because Congress, in its infinite wisdom, decided that a married couple should be treated as a single economic unit and be permitted to postpone taxation until the death of the surviving spouse. Having the tax postponed until the second spouse's death allows the family to shift assets and invest the money to produce income and capital appreciation. It is a valuable tool for married couples, but the law does not give a similar tax break to single, widowed, or divorced persons, or spouses that are not U.S. citizens.

In order to qualify for the deduction (it is not automatic), property must actually pass to the surviving spouse. This can include property passing outside your will as long as it is part of your gross estate. For example, half of jointly owned property with rights of survivorship and proceeds from life insurance, in which you name your spouse beneficiary of any life insurance proceeds (without conditions) and give to the survivor total control over the unpaid proceeds, qualify. If the spouse is *not* given total control, then the proceeds are paid to the estate and they then become taxable. This most important condition—giving the survivor total control—must be met in order to qualify for the marital deduction.

The purpose in this chapter has been to familiarize you with the tax implications of estate planning and how it can effect you and your family. But everyone doesn't pay estate tax. Most estates, as a matter of fact, will pay little or nothing to the government because the property in the estate will pass to the surviving spouse tax-free. Even if there is no spouse, up to the $600,000 lifetime exemption equivalent can be used to escape estate taxes.

Although the imposition of gift and estate taxes on individuals produces a relatively small percentage of all revenues received by the government during any one year, it can create hardships to many families because of reduced incomes at a time when the money is most needed. All the more reason that your diligence as an estate planner should be most welcome, especially by those who will be recipients of your efforts. Yes, there are tax restraints placed on property transfers, and perhaps the current tax rates are high in the minds of many. But the government does allow you to take advantage of its laws to reduce tax liability. It is up to you to do the rest.

4

Creating a Trust for Tax Savings

Over 130 years ago Oliver Wendell Holmes, the great jurist, said, "Put not your trust in money, but put your money in trusts." Holmes was aware, even in his day, how valuable a financial and tax-saving instrument a trust was. It still is. But people, for years, have avoided the use of trusts because trusts appear to be mysterious and complex legal instruments. Indeed, any trust instrument can be complicated. You really should have a lawyer trained in estate and tax planning to handle its implementation. Trusts, taxes, and estate financial planning are all interrelated. Certain trusts can help you pass assets and property to the next generation, and perhaps future generations, and in addition reduce your estate taxes. Others are less costly to create and administer but do not reduce tax liability. At the same time, a trust allows your estate to go directly to your heirs without having to go through the costly and time-consuming process of a probate proceeding.

Indeed, establishing a trust can be useful to you in planning your estate. If you are the kind of busy person who can spend very little time in managing your properties, investments and other financial affairs, it can help. If you need to be assured that your loved ones will be taken care of if you become sick or after you die, then you should consider a trust instrument. If you want to set up an education fund for children or grandchildren and have professionals manage the investments, certainly a trust can be used to good advantage. If you would like to gift some money to your college or charity and receive income from the gift during your life, a trust instrument can be used. In employing a trust instrument for your long-term estate planning goals, it would be wise to show great care in considering the needs and requirements of those persons named in the trust. It is a contract where you agree to turn over your assets to the trust and the trustee contracts to invest or otherwise hold the assets for the benefit of those named as beneficiaries.

The use of trusts is not a new development. They were employed over 500 years ago in England and established in common law to protect property and family when the owner went away and left his castle and other properties "in trust" for his family. The overall objective of trusts now is to accomplish somewhat the same purpose and, in addition, reduce the tax liability of assets left in the estate of the deceased. There are many types of trusts in use today. They provide people from all economic classes with the flexibility to accommodate changing conditions, the management of trust assets, and the insurance of property transfer at death.

What is a trust and how can it help you in your estate planning?

A trust is an arrangement and a device in which legal title to an asset is transferred from the owner (grantor-trustor) to one or more persons, a bank or a trust company, or another entity to manage and control property for the benefit of others. The grantor must put an intention in writing to convey the property and to impose duties on the part of the trustees to effectively manage the assets or property of the trust for the specific benefit of those named in the trust agreement. This situation implies fiduciary responsibility in which trustees are subject to the "rule of the prudent man" in investing and managing securities that are in the trust.

Creating a Trust

When you create a trust you can establish your own rules as to how the trust will operate subject to the legal limitations and constraints placed on trusts by the individual states. Most states require that you (1) state the purpose of the trust, (2) give a description of the properties that it will contain, (3) mention the length of time it will last, and (4) list the names of the beneficiaries, how much they will acquire in assets, what they will receive in property (real or personal), and when it will be received.

Every trust should be in writing with clear and unambiguous language and must have specified intent. As the grantor, you have to list the property that you place into the trust and it must be referred to precisely and clearly. The property can include your residence, a vacation home, an office building, an apartment house, a farm, bank accounts, stocks, bonds, mutual funds, insurance, the family business, and cash, copyrights, or patents, among other things. In addition to it having a valid purpose, the trust must not violate the laws of public policy and must satisfy the terms of the trust and see that other specific conditions are met by the named beneficiaries set forth in the document before the transfer of any property to beneficiaries takes place. Also, if, in its language, the trust attempts to deprive the spouse, for instance, of marital rights, either inadvertently or not, it can be declared invalid. However, before going on in our discussion of trusts, let us look at some of the active players involved in trust creation and maintenance.

The Grantor

The grantor is the individual who is the creator of the trust and who places assets into the trust in the form of real or personal property, cash, or other assets either currently or at some later date. Other names for the grantor are trustor, donor, maker, or settlor. The grantor must have the legal authority to control, convey, and distribute assets to another. In order to do this he or she must be legally competent to do so. If the person happens to be a minor, is incompetent, or is proved to be mentally unstable, then that person cannot legally convey property to another.

The Trustee

The trust document allows the trustee(s) to have a legal interest in the property by holding title to the assets, managing them, and then distributing principal and income as directed by the trust document. A trustee can be, for example, a person(s) or an institution, such as a bank, a trust company, a mutual fund, a brokerage firm, or a law firm. The powers given to the trustee are spelled out in the trust instrument, and sometimes the arrangements for distribution and payment schedules to beneficiaries can be very complex. Even statements regarding the use of the trustee's own judgment can be specified and made part of the document. Periodic reports to all interested parties must be made, including those to beneficiaries. The trustee must pay necessary bills, deposit income, keep records of securities transactions and remove the responsibility of the financial and administrative management from the grantor and beneficiaries.

Provisions must also be made in the trust agreement that, in the event the trustee dies, becomes incapacitated, or is unable to manage the trust effectively, a successor trustee be designated, but only after appropriate medical examinations and conclusions as to incapacity of the original trustee are attested to. If, for any reason, the trust document does not specify a successor trustee, the court will appoint one. In addition, the trustee cannot use any of the trust property for his or her own purposes. If the trust document is prepared by the bank or trust company, it may give itself too many powers. What are the duties and obligations of the trustee? What is expected of him or her so far as management of assets are concerned? What are the rights and duties of the beneficiary? What are the trustee fees and other costs? These must be discussed in advance.

Especially important is the financial management of the assets in the trust. It would behoove you to select a person whom you know has the ability and a degree of competence in the area of investing and money management to protect the trust principal and have the value of the assets grow over the years. Your trustee can be a close relative or a friend, but you should be very diligent in choosing the right person or institution for that position.

Cotrustee

A living trust can also be drawn naming a cotrustee(s) to assist you as trustee, or a named trustee in managing the trust. A generally condoned practice by some lawyers is to suggest to the grantor that he or she name a particular trust company or bank that the estate planning lawyer has a relationship with and has worked with as a cotrustee before. This type of working arrangement can be extremely satisfying because it will go a long way in removing some of the stress and time consumed in finding and selecting an appropriate cotrustee for you. It also eliminates the need to choose a relative or friend with sufficient investment management experience to handle your assets. The corporate cotrustee has the background to do it.

Successor Trustee

A successor trustee would be a person, a bank, or a trust company appointed by you to replace yourself or an original trustee when either of you cannot continue to serve for any reason. Or the successor can be the one you name who takes over for you after you die, manages your trust assets, and then turns the trust property over to the named beneficiaries under the conditions stated in the trust document.

Beneficiary

A beneficiary can be a person(s), an institution, a charity, or a for-profit corporation that can receive property, income earnings interest, or principal from the trust. Some are considered the primary beneficiaries, such as the surviving spouse, children, and grandchildren. Others would be secondary or tertiary beneficiaries. There is no specific formula as to what a primary beneficiary might receive as a percentage of the entire estate. Some primary beneficiaries have been known to receive a token bequest. In most cases, however, the primary beneficiaries suffer no such inequities and, if such a thing did happen, it probably would not escape judicial review. If you decide to disinherit a primary beneficiary, you must state the name or names of those persons very clearly so the court will be clear as to who is and who is not included in your estate plan. Your attorney should definitely have a record of the reasons for your decision to prevent any challenge to the will or trust.

This discussion of trusts has defined some of the people and/or institutions that are involved in the utilization of a trust instrument. Let us explain first the revocable living trust—one that has become popular over the years, and then describe why it has.

The Revocable Living Trust

The revocable living trust is a document that, when properly drafted, can provide you and your family with income during the time you are alive and then have someone other than yourself handle your financial affairs when you cannot, or choose not to. Basically, the key to this form of trust allows you, as grantor, to act as your own trustee or to make provisions to turn over the assets to a financial institution such as a bank, a trust company, or to a named individual that can act as a sole trustee, as a cotrustee, or as a successor trustee. The trust instrument will instruct the trustee(s) what to do with the trust property during the grantor's lifetime.

A living trust is one that is created during your lifetime and it can be revocable or irrevocable. The former can be revoked or altered at a specific date or at any time. The grantor has the right to change the terms of the trust, including the names of the beneficiaries, the amounts they are to receive, and the way in which they are benefited. After the death of the grantor the revocable trust can continue to have efficacy and will remain intact to provide income to beneficiaries according to the document, or it can be terminated, with property being distributed to named beneficiaries.

Who would need a living trust and what are its advantages? Although living trusts can be employed by people in every tax bracket, those who are attracted to this device are those in the middle class who have a small-to medium-sized estate between $750,000 and $3,000,000, generally are married, and have some children and perhaps grandchildren.

Some Advantages of the Revocable Living Trust

- Your estate will not be subject to probate, administrative expenses or delays involving distribution of assets and other personal or real property to your beneficiaries.
- You can revoke the trust at any time. And you may also change the contents of the trust whenever you are dissatisfied with the way it works. This freedom and flexibility make it a very useful estate planning tool.
- A trust can unify assets in one account and provide professional management of assets.
- If you act as your own trustee and manage your own investments, there are no fees until a financial institution or private money manager takes over.
- A trust can collect life insurance proceeds, with little lost time, to help pay for immediate post-mortem expenses.
- It can provide, after you die, financial support for a dependent spouse and children or mentally or physically disabled dependents.
- Probate *costs*, which can add up to between 5–7 percent of your probated estate, can be substantially reduced or eliminated.
- If you become incompetent and are not able to make sound managerial and financial decisions, the trust can provide for management without any influence from the courts or other parties.

- A trust can provide for the disposition of assets in a more confidential way as compared to a will, which is a matter of public record. It may, however, become public if someone objects to the terms of the trust.
- A trust can oversee and administer the receipt of inheritance monies for underage children before they are mature enough to manage the assets themselves.
- It can protect your property from some beneficiaries who are inclined to be irresponsible or otherwise unable to manage property that they receive by will.
- *Valid* creditor claims against your estate after death and the payment of certain questioned expense items are more likely to be disposed of quickly because of less court involvement and judicial supervision.

If you decide to have professional trust management, you can determine how well a bank trust company or other manager performs while you are still alive and can make any necessary changes if you are not satisfied.

Property Must Be Retitled

Establishing a revocable living trust requires that property currently owned by you and to become trust property must be retitled before it can be legally owned by the trust. For instance, the names that are presently on the certificates of stocks, bonds, and other securities will have to be retitled to indicate new ownership and to be reissued in the name of the trust. If all securities are held "in street name" by a stock brokerage house, this retitling is not required. A copy of the trust document, however, is required to be given to the securities firm and recorded. Your monthly brokerage statements would reflect the change, showing the name of the trust, the trustee, and the date it was formed.

If you do not have your securities located at a stock brokerage firm and instead keep the actual certificates in a safety deposit box or at home, you will have to either have your attorney handle the retitling or do it yourself. You can send a copy of the trust agreement (signed by you on the back of the certificate) to the transfer agent of each company in which you hold shares of stock, allowing the agent to retitle the certificates. This can be a great deal of work if you own a lot of shares of stock. You really should allow a stock brokerage firm to do it. If you don't have an account, open one, deposit the securities with it and provide its representative with a valid copy of the trust agreement. There may or may not be a small fee involved, but you will have accomplished your goal with very little difficulty. If the property to be transferred to the trust is real estate, you have to legally assign the property to the trust. The trust would then be responsible for the debt service, the payment of property taxes, and insurance, among other things. It would also receive the income, if any, that the property generates.

Standby or Takeover Trust

Another type of revocable trust—the standby trust—should be considered in your estate planning because, together with the pour-over will, it can significantly help unify your estate. The pour-over provision in your will transfers all or a portion of your assets into a preexisting revocable living trust to be distributed with other assets mentioned in the trust document. The *standby trust* complements this pour-over provision and gives the grantor the satisfaction that the property is immediately managed after death occurs. It is generally established for those persons who have a will but find it difficult to sign away any powers during their lifetime or to enter into any agreement in which they must relinquish control over their assets to a trustee, even if the trust happens to be revocable. This reluctance is easily understood, and for this kind of person the standby arrangement may work very well because it allows the transfer of a minimal amount of assets with the option of adding more from time to time at the grantor's option. Most kinds of property can be placed under the umbrella of a standby trust: tangible personal property, such as furniture, clothing, a car, real estate, etc.

If and when the need arises (the grantor becomes incapacitated, mentally ill, or senile), the estate can be protected through the use of a predesignated successor trustee previously selected by the grantor, who can "under certain conditions" assume control of the estate's physical properties and financial assets in addition to the general affairs of the grantor. Prior to the actual takeover by the successor trustee, a custodial arrangement can be established in which the trustee administers limited duties, such as safekeeping of securities or some bookkeeping. The standby trust allows the grantor full control of the estate while he or she is able to manage it, and then it protects the grantor when it becomes obvious that he or she cannot remain in that capacity.

If the grantor has several trusts, the pour-over will provision must also identify which trust is to be the recipient of the assets. In addition, it should be remembered that although pour-over clauses in wills are useful, they cannot protect assets that are left out of the trust from going through probate. Thus, if you are very sick with little hope of recovery, it is best to make the transfer of assets out of your estate and into the trust. If you recover you have the flexibility to reverse your decision.

The question is often raised why it is necessary to also

have a will if one has a trust. A will is necessary because there is always a strong possibility that some of your property will not be titled under the trust. Some property may be in the process of being poured into the trust but not yet legally owned as trust property. In that case, without a will and not under a trust, the property is unprotected and your will must fall in all likelihood under the jurisdiction of the court. The pour-over provision is essential if these assets are to be poured in and retitled as trust property.

The assets that are transferred into a revocable trust are not considered to be completed gifts for federal tax purposes because you did not give this property away irrevocably. Consequently, there is no tax liability. But there are also no estate tax advantages. You, as grantor, still retain control over the property and are required to pay income tax and capital gains tax, if any, under your tax identification number. Upon death, the corpus (the entire body of your property) would be subject to estate tax liability.

Trusts, like wills, are recognized as valid legal instruments in every state and the District of Columbia. If you move from one state to another, few if any changes in your agreement would be required for validation.

Disadvantages Associated with a Revocable Living Trust

- Time, effort, and sometimes transfer fees are usually required to transfer assets into the name of a trust.
- Creditor claims may not be cut off as quickly as under a will. Creditors are permitted to make claims, whether valid or not, against trust assets long after most properties have been distributed to heirs. This can drag on and may turn out to be costly.

- A trust that is revocable does not save you estate taxes and does not shelter you from income taxes that you would have had to pay if there had not been a trust arrangement.
- Fees for trust supervision and investment management must be paid if you are not the active trustee yourself.
- You will have to pay an attorney for preparing the trust document.
- A trust cannot make arrangements for the distribution of assets that are *not* trust property.

Testamentary Trusts

Unlike the living trust created during one's lifetime, testamentary trusts are initiated and established under the terms of a will. These trusts do not benefit you as a grantor in any way and have no efficacy while you are alive. They benefit only those persons whose property the trust becomes after you die. A testamentary trust can be established to provide the same degree of flexibility that an earlier established living trust provides, in which income and earnings from trust assets are accumulated and disbursed at the discretion of the trustee or sprinkled to a variety of beneficiaries as the trust document stipulates. The trustee may also hold both principal and interest for distribution at some later date for the benefit of named beneficiaries.

This type of trust can also be drafted to protect minors and other family members who might be incapable of taking care of their own financial affairs. If, for instance, a twenty-one-year-old is considered immature and should not be left a large sum of money at your death, the trustee can pay out small sums as needed so the whole amount will not be squandered in a short period of time.

Guidelines can be established in the trust document by the use of a "spendthrift clause" that will prohibit a beneficiary who has uncontrollable spending habits from transferring or selling his or her rights to trust property. The clause states, in effect, that "no interest of the beneficiaries of this trust shall be transferable or assignable, or subject to any claims by creditors of the beneficiary. The spendthrift provisions of the trust need to be worded in such a way that the rights of the donee to the property are severely limited so that creditors have little recourse in attempting to acquire something that the donee doesn't have. If, however, once the property is received by the donee, then it is no longer protected from creditors. Spendthrift provisions (or spendthrift trusts when the trust is set up independently and not as part of a broader living or testamentary trust) are valid in many states, but not all.

The Irrevocable Trust

The irrevocable trust has all the advantages of the living trust mentioned previously, but it is less a device merely to escape probate costs and more of an outright gift of property that cannot be returned to you. Management of the trust is usually lodged in someone other than yourself and very careful consideration must be given to any retention of powers by you as grantor that may be construed to establish even the slightest control over the management of the assets and other properties in the trust. If this were the case, it might lead to tax consequence liability. Indeed, once an irrevocable trust is established, the grantor cannot amend, revoke, or in any way alter the agreement to have the corpus revert to himself or herself. Any power over the corpus to alter or modify the interests of the beneficiaries would also be substantially limited. It would, therefore, behoove you as grantor to allow another person, bank, or trust company to become trustee. Admittedly, you have lost control over the property, but you save on income taxes because the trust transfers the tax liability of those in higher brackets to those within the family who are in lower tax brackets.

Although the grantor must make a completed gift of property over which he or she will lose control and will not receive the income that the asset produces, there is good and sufficient purpose for the irrevocable transfer: it removes income and possible capital appreciation from the grantor's estate, and it also reduces the total value of assets subject to estate tax liability that remain in the gross estate. If your taxable estate exceeds the $600,000 lifetime exemption equivalent, it would be a good idea to transfer at least enough property into an irrevocable trust to reduce the value of your estate below this level. By doing this, you will be avoiding any estate tax liability and taking full advantage of the unified credit. You can place any type of property in the irrevocable trust, but assets producing high yields, income-oriented mutual funds, certificates of deposit, dividend-paying stocks, bonds, and even savings accounts are the most preferable items to place in an irrevocable trust. The assets need to produce income. If they fail to do this, then not very much will be saved in taxes. Remember, the point is to shift income from you, the grantor, to the trust and have it build up outside your estate.

An irrevocable trust agreement can cause problems for you if you are not sure about what you would like to accomplish, especially if you place too much of your net worth into the trust as a completed irrevocable gift and later find out that you are confronted with a substantial financial emergency that you could not have anticipated. So it would be prudent to strike some kind of balance. You need to retain sufficient property in your own name or in a revocable trust to maintain your current standard of living for as long as you believe you and your spouse might live. Then you must measure those assets against the ones you can place into the irrevocable trust because you will not be legally able to have control over the irrevocable trust property ever again.

It is true that irrevocable trusts can dramatically reduce your tax liability. But you can effectively wipe out any tax advantage that you may acquire through errors in drafting the trust document or inadvertently by your own action. The money and other assets in the trust would then revert to your estate and be taxed accordingly. For example, income from the trust cannot be used to discharge any legal obligations owed by you as the grantor, nor can it be employed to support any person or entity that you have a legal responsibility to support, like your parental or spousal responsibilities regarding food, clothing, medical care, etc. Also, if life insurance premiums are paid with trust income on your life as the insured, the amounts paid will generally be taxed to you personally.

The grantor generally cannot reserve any "incidents of ownership" over trust assets. An irrevocable trust, however, will allow you, the grantor, to be your own trustee, but the powers that may be retained by you would be severely limited and cannot go beyond mere administration of the trust. If you, for instance, reserve the right to change beneficiaries in the trust document, it might also be suspect. Having an independent trustee, therefore, would be more appropriate and indicate a relinquishing of power and control by you over trust assets.

The Distribution of Assets

How, when, and in what manner the assets are distributed to the named beneficiaries is decided originally by the grantor and then by trustee(s) or others who are named to handle trust property. Income from trust assets is permitted to accumulate over the years, but taxes must be paid. Proper management of resources requires that distributions be paid out under specific arrangement directed by the trust instrument. It may be a triggering event, such as a commencement from college, a birthday, a wedding, or the birth of a child. It also can take place when the value of the trust builds up to a specific amount or on a particular date. Trust income, or principal, can be paid to named beneficiaries and may be in the form of a lump-sum distribution after monies have accumulated over a period of years. Or, payments can be made to beneficiaries on a weekly or monthly basis for the purpose of providing the person(s) with a steady income stream. These periodic distributions usually go to dependent spouses, minor children, or incompetent individuals, with the money given for such designated purposes as clothing, food, education, or to provide shelter. It cannot be used for any other purpose. Arrangements for periodic distributions under this type of financial support can be written into a living testamentary trust arrangement with payments to start after your death.

Powers of Appointment

Earlier in the chapter the duties were discussed of the trustee or successor trustee, depending on the wording of the trust document, those implied by law, and others granted by statute: collecting and holding property, investing and managing assets and money, among other things. The grantor, if he or she wishes, can provide additional powers to the trustee through the issuance of powers of appointment. The grantor says I empower another after I die to make certain decisions regarding my estate that I cannot make now, so I give the power to the holder whom I name, the right to dispose of trust property and to change beneficiaries named under the trust agreement. The one receiving the power is called a donee and is permitted a great deal of latitude and flexibility under a general power of appointment. This latitude and flexibility can be necessary in certain family situations in which, after a period of years, circumstances change and therefore old arrangements must be altered and new requirements must be addressed. The "general power" can allow for postmortem flexibility, but it can also be so broad as to allow the donee to give property to himself or herself or anyone else that the donee chooses. On the contrary, if a "limited power" is given, then the property is prohibited from going to the donee, the creditors, or the estate of the donee. A trustee may acquire increased powers over trust affairs even though the grantor might not have approved of the action while he or she was alive, by petitioning the probate court. This action, if successful, would substantially reduce any challenges by dissatisfied beneficiaries.

A power that has been employed successfully in recent years is known as a "sprinkling arrangement," sometimes called a "sprinkling trust." Because most persons, when they establish a trust, cannot predict the future needs of beneficiaries, a trust with a sprinkling arrangement gives the trustee discretionary powers to spray income in a flexible way when needed. Suppose, for example, a trust is created with income payable to three grandchildren in certain amounts to be determined by the trustee. One of the grandchildren, after graduating from medical school, needs $30,000 to begin a medical practice. The father of the graduate, who didn't do much estate planning on his own regarding his three sons, asks the trustee(s) to give him the money so he can then give it to his son at what he considers the appropriate time.

But, in all probability, the father would be taxed on the receipt of the money even though he would be acting merely as a conduit. If the trust had sprinkling powers, it would be better to pay the money directly to the grandchild, and the grandchild would pay a tax on the income at an appreciably lower tax rate.

How Long Can a Trust Last?

The current rule that governs and controls how long a trust can be made to last is called the "Rule against Perpetuities." It prohibits anyone from maintaining family control and distribution of property from the current generation to future generations. More specifically, the rule states that a trust cannot own or control property for longer than the life in being named in the trust, plus twenty-one years. Beyond such a time, the property must vest and beneficiaries must receive full rights of ownership. To protect you from the possibility of violating this rule, be sure the following clause is included in your trust instrument. The language is as follows:

> . . . the trust created herein that has not been terminated sooner, shall terminate twenty-one (21) years after the death of the last survivor of the class composed of (use the grantor's name here) and those of the grantor's children or grandchildren and "others" who are still living on the day of my death.

Combining a Will and a Trust

If you are the one who receives the authority under a trust, you need to coordinate what is stated regarding the transference of property in a duly drawn and executed will and the assets that are to be transferred under a trust. It would be wise to have the same attorney draw both instruments. If, for instance, the trust were drafted first and the will executed at some later date and the will had no residuary clause that automatically exercises a power of appointment, then it is possible that the trust property can fall under the provisions of the will unless it is specifically stated that it does not. Therefore, the will and the trust have to be coordinated so that naming certain beneficiaries and including specific provisions regarding the disposition of assets does not later result in any loss of assets to intended beneficiaries or unexpected costs to the estate.

State Laws Regarding Trusts

You probably will not find much information on state laws that govern the way trusts operate. Most states have adopted, among other codes, the *Uniform Probate Code* and the *Uniform Trustees Powers Act,* which reduce the time and cost of research. These laws outline what trustees may or may not do, what trustees may charge for services, and whether or not they are required to post bond (insurance) if trust funds should be stolen. In addition, states have laws regarding the appointment of out-of-state trustees and trustee registration as to the trust entity and to themselves as trustees. In most states, creditor's rights vary regarding claiming and reaching beneficiaries' income.

There also appears to be little uniformity among state transfer systems and, by extension, in the composition of estate taxes. Many states impose the maximum amount the federal tax law allows a state to take as a dollar-for-dollar credit against federal taxes. Nearly all states levy a "credit estate tax" or a "pick-up tax" designed to absorb the amount of the federal estate tax credit allowed for taxes paid to the state. In some jurisdictions, however, there is no state death tax unless there is a federal estate tax. Others may impose a state inheritance tax or an estate tax where there is no federal tax. Because of variations in how states handle taxes on the transfer of property, tax rates, and exemptions, you should check with the State Department of Revenue and Taxation of your particular state to ascertain what your overall tax liability will be.

Filings for Trusts

If you have a revocable trust, no separate income tax filing is required. You can indicate on your #1040 federal tax form that a trust exists, the date it was formed and the name of the trustee, but it is not necessary. An irrevocable trust, however, requires a separate identification number, and each year a fiduciary tax return and federal and state income tax returns must be filed. As a separate and distinct entity, the irrevocable trust is treated like a single person and is therefore subject to essentially the same exclusions and exemptions to reduce reportable income received by the trust as a person is.

Deposit Insurance for Trusts

Trust accounts that are placed in a bank and deposited under the provisions of a revocable living trust are insured as an individual's funds, but they will be added to any other single ownership account that you as depositor have at the bank. Consequently, the total amount your funds can be insured for is $100,000, the maximum insurance provided by the Federal Insurance Deposit Corporation (FDIC). Funds of a revocable trust can be separately insured and distinguished from the grantor's own funds, but must meet special requirements that are applicable to what can be described as "testamentary" accounts. Notably, the account must clearly evidence intentions that the funds shall belong to a named beneficiary upon the death of the grantor-depositor. These accounts are sometimes known as Totten Trust accounts or POD accounts.* The requirements for separate coverage are very specific and should be discussed with your banking or trust officer.

Irrevocable trust accounts, on the other hand, constitute a separate and distinct legal ownership and entity. The interest of each beneficiary named in the trust agreement is insured up to $100,000 separately and from other accounts held by the depositor-grantor trustee or beneficiary. But specific requirements must be met for this separate insurance. Furthermore, if the beneficiary has an ownership interest in more than one trust created by the same grantor, the interests of that beneficiary in all accounts are added together and the sum of the accounts are insured to a maximum of $100,000.

Trusts Are Unique and Flexible Instruments

The use of trusts requires the transfer of monies out of your name and into a trust. Think in terms of a transfer amount that will be sufficient (including any possible capital appreciation) to pay any projected estate taxes at your death. If it is irrevocable, never transfer more property than you believe would be prudent, and transfer only an amount that will allow you to maintain your current life style. Also, consider a property transfer that would reduce the size of your taxable estate to the

---

*These are discussed in Chapter 10.

$1,200,000 exemption equivalent for both spouses, or $600,000 for one at about the age of life expectancy.

Trusts are a unique and very useful arrangement embodying a plethora of legal principals and relationships involving current estate tax law. But almost every trust is based on the same overall concept: a relationship is established in which one person or institution holds legal title to assets during a period of time for the use and benefit of another. Trusts are managed by trustees, either individual or corporate, with income and sometimes principal distributed in accordance with the purposes and provisions stated in the trust document. Most important, trusts are very flexible, and any donor can have a trust designed to achieve any estate planning goal as long as it follows legal guidelines. But rules and regulations that govern the establishment and maintenance of a trust require experience in the law. Nearly every year there are attempts by individuals and organizations to exploit any possible loopholes in the law and use them for their own purposes. However, it is not as easy to do this as it once was because the government is periodically altering current regulations, passing new laws, and issuing tougher compliance regulations. This discipline requires precise legal language and a great familiarity with the constantly changing tax code. To draft a complicated trust document on your own can create monumental problems for you and your family and may very well negate whatever you as the grantor-donor wish to accomplish.

This chapter has shown that a trust can be an efficient and effective way to make certain that your property reaches your intended heirs. The modern trust instrument has evolved to capture the current legal and estate tax developments that make it an attractive vehicle for estate tax planning. Indeed, certain trusts can save taxes while you are alive and can protect your estate and beneficiaries after you die. But in order for the trust to become a workable and effective legal tool, you have to decide what you want to accomplish by creating it. Who do you wish to benefit, and under what circumstances would this be accomplished? Some time and effort on your part will need to be applied.

5

Marital and Generation-Skipping Trusts

There are, as we have learned, several benefits that can accrue to you in employing a trust instrument for your estate planning. One is achieving estate tax savings. Another, is avoiding the costs and the time-consuming nature of the probate process. But perhaps a more important feature of the trust instrument is its aiding you as the grantor in passing as much property as is legally possible, tax free, to your spouse and children, among others. Wealth retention and tax reduction strategies may on their face appear to be a simple solution for most people, but in many cases the first spouse will leave too much in assets to the second spouse outright, thus inadvertently and unintentionally creating a tax problem for the survivor. Unless the second spouse finds a way to reduce the amount of assets that now make up his or her estate, substantial liability can occur at the survivor's death. In this chapter, then, a type of trust will be considered that can be employed by married couples when their combined assets are in excess of $600,000. Here, each spouse becomes part of a split-trust arrangement, and each can legally take advantage of the $600,000 lifetime exemption. This type of trust is known as an A-B trust, but it is also commonly called a bypass trust, a family trust, and a credit shelter trust. The A-B-C trust discussed later in the chapter is also referred to as a Q-tip trust, where Q-tip stands for "qualified terminal interest property." Both the A-B and the A-B-C trusts work with each other and can be constructed under a will, or a living trust arrangement during, the grantor's lifetime.

A-B or Bypass Trust

Usually employed by married couples, the purpose of establishing the A-B or bypass trust is to provide financial security to the surviving spouse, to take advantage of each spouse's lifetime exemption equivalent, and to pass property to children and other beneficiaries without paying estate taxes. To initiate this type of trust, it is best to start with the drafting of a revocable living trust (later referred to as the master trust) that has combined assets of both the husband and wife of an assumed amount of $1,200,000. This living trust continues its life while the husband and wife are alive but is not identified as an A-B trust until the first spouse dies. At that time, this master trust is divided in half to become two subtrusts, one of which shall be called the "A" trust and the other, the "B" trust. The A part becomes the survivor's trust and is now the sole property of the surviving spouse. An amount of $600,000, equal to one half of the total value of trust assets in the master trust is transferred into the A subtrust, which will provide benefits for the exclusive use of the surviving spouse. The trust assets will legally bypass the survivor's estate at some later date and escape all tax liability, providing there is no increase in the value of the net taxable estate above the exemption amount.

The other, B half of the original combined estate becomes the decedent's trust. It is designed to preserve, as much as possible, the *deceased* spouse's lifetime exemption equivalent from estate taxes. By transferring one half of the original amount into the B sub-trust, both spouses can now effectively take advantage of the $600,000 exemption limit. The funds will be invested in assets with an income component, and the surviving spouse can now receive an additional stream of income from the B trust. All ownership rights to the property will eventually pass, however, to the children or other named beneficiaries after the second spouse's death.

The surviving spouse has complete control over the A trust and no one, not even a prospective beneficiary or the courts, have anything to say about its use. How the money or assets are used and how they are disposed of is strictly a private matter. The survivor is required, however, to keep records, for income tax purposes, and report the receipt of all income dividends, and capital gains. The other part of the Master Trust, the decedent's of B trust, allows the surviving spouse to have all the income from the trust and the right to receive up to 5 percent of the trust principal each year. The trustee is generally given the right to make distributions of principal under extraordinary circumstances, especially in areas such as health, education, and support and maintenance of the survivor. There are no courts or attorneys to interfere with what is done, and the ultimate beneficiaries, generally the children of the marriage, are not involved in any way. Assets are drawn from the trust when requested. Remember, the surviving spouse, usually the wife because of a history of longer longevity, is the trustee of trust A and may also be the successor trustee of the B trust. She can decide on her own whether or not the income she receives from the A trust is sufficient to maintain her in an acceptable life style. Can the ultimate beneficiaries complain that the monies in the trust are being drained or used indiscriminately and will eventually be dissipated? Of course, but they are not likely to do so. Evidence suggests that most people do not suddenly change their lifestyles or intentionally deplete assets when they have the ability to do so.

In a somewhat similar situation, let's say that assets invested and titled in your name alone give you a gross estate of $900,000. Your eventual purpose is to have an amount equal to your $600,000 lifetime exemption equivalent go to your son without any tax liability. But you would also like the principal to be used so your wife will receive the income from the investments until she dies. You can create a bypass Trust by placing $600,000 in assets into the trust when you die and naming your wife as income beneficiary and having your son receive the remainder interest. The $300,000 that remains in your estate and is not placed into the trust is given to your wife, without any conditions, at your death. So the $600,000 passes tax free and the remaining $300,000 of net worth qualifies as a tax free unlimited marital deduction. No gift tax is paid on the transfer. Eventually this $300,000 plus another $300,000 that has been personally held by your wife and is part of her estate, becomes taxable at her death, but is exempt from estate taxes because she still retains her $600,000 lifetime exemption equivalent. In effect, your wife not only receives the income from B trust while she is alive, but additional income from her own investments. The principal from the B trust goes directly to your son free from any estate tax.

If, for instance, a bypass trust were not created, but instead the husband employed the unlimited marital deduction alone and just gave his entire $900,000 net worth to his wife, at her death the wife would have to pay estate tax on the original unprotected $600,000 that belonged to her late husband plus on the additional $300,000 that she received as part of the unlimited marital deduction. In addition, the other $300,000 in her name would be taxed. This would make a total of 1.2 million subject to estate tax, assuming no increase or decrease in the total. After she received a lifetime exemption equivalent on her own $600,000 ($300,000 + $300,000) an estate tax would be levied on the remaining $600,000. This could have been avoided by the use of a bypass trust. So it would behoove the grantor to use the marital deduction discriminatingly and prudently. Its misuse can have dire tax implications.

Assets, to the extent they *exceed* the $600,000 estate tax equivalent, are subject to estate taxes. Income from the trust assets is taxed to the trust under federal and perhaps state income tax rules. Whatever is not taxed is left to grow in the B trust and when the surviving spouse dies and the assets, including after-tax accumulated income, go to the beneficiaries, no estate tax liability is incurred. Hence, the use of the A-B trust concept is effective because it minimizes tax liabilities and also because it allows a married couple to avoid having their estate diminished so as to leave a substantial sum to their beneficiaries. The A-B trust can be created during your life as a living trust, or it can be established under your will as a testamentary trust. It is preferable to do it while you are living so the lifetime exemption equivalent of $600,000 will escape probate.

Funding a Trust by Disclaimer to Reduce Taxes

A method of equalizing your estate through tax reduction can be employed by the use of the disclaimer. It involves the establishment of an A-B (bypass) trust. Usually, trusts are funded with assets that produce income. Here, in the wills of each spouse, everything is left to the other, with provisions that any property that the survivor legitimately disclaims will go into an existing A-B trust. Although the surviving spouse can, if the needs are present, accept the property that is available currently, the survivor, however, can also "disclaim." By refusing the bequest, the property can go through to the trust, and the husband and wife team are able to fund a trust and have the assets later bypass the survivor's estate without any tax being assessed. Disclaimers, however, must follow certain rules and regulations in order to be legal. Most importantly, the disclaimer must be irrevocable, in writing, and the person must unconditionally refuse to accept the property. In addition, the trustee must have received notice of the disclaimer within nine months of the decedent's death. Using the disclaimer mechanism gives the combined spouses a great deal of flexibility because the trusts can be funded up to the lifetime exemption equivalent amounts. If the second spouse is not likely to die too long after the first spouse, and if they work as a team, they can disclaim a sufficient amount of inherited property to lower tax-brackets on both estates through equalization.

A-B-C Trust

The A-B-C trust adds another dimension to the A-B trust and is commonly known as a "qualified terminable interest property (Q-tip)." It came into being as part of the 1981 tax act. Its primary importance is allowing the first spouse, even after death, to control, through stated provisions in the trust document, not only the management of trust assets but also their final disposition and distribution after the death of the second spouse. Its function also is to pour assets into a "C" trust when the A-B trust has used up both exemption equivalents and there still is money or other assets that would be subject to taxation.

The A-B-C trust or Q-tip must provide for the surviving

spouse to be paid all the income earned by the trust each year, thus creating a marital life estate during the surviving spouse's lifetime. As the one who can be the trust's only beneficiary, the survivor has a definite interest in what takes place in trust management and oversight. The survivor has a right to remove all income that the trust generates and to satisfy any basic needs. If there is a greater need for income than what the trust generates, because of increased living expenses or for what can be described as requirements for health, education, support, and maintenance of the survivor, the trustee will generally allow the Q-tip principal to be invaded. But, if it is invaded, the reduction of principal could very well diminish the total amount of funds being invested and reinvested and reduce the level of trust income. On the other hand, removal of funds would at some later date reduce the size of the survivor's estate that is subject to taxes.

Also, the principal as Q-tip property may not be used to support anyone other than the surviving spouse. Property placed into a Q-tip can qualify for the unlimited marital deduction only after a proper election is made by the trustee (or executor) after the death of the first spouse. If Q-tip property is used to support anyone other than the surviving spouse, it would disqualify the use of the marital deduction and subject the survivor to further estate tax. Furthermore, the legal rights accorded a Q-tip and given to the survivor do not last forever. They survive only until death. Additionally, the survivor's terminable interest cannot be transferred to anyone else. This is to insure that the trust assets are included in the survivor's estate.

How does the A-B-C trust work? In an earlier description of an A-B or master living revocable trust, there was placed $1,200,000 in assets titled under the trust prior to the death of the first spouse. When the first spouse dies the property in the master trust is split into two subtrusts in which $600,000 goes into the A trust, the survivor's trust, and $600,000 is placed into the B trust (bypass) or decedent's trust. The combined estate is not assessed any tax liability because each spouse is able to utilize his and her full lifetime exemption equivalents under current law. Adding a C trust, which can be funded with assets in excess of the exemption limit, can essentially delay estate tax liability until the surviving spouse dies. If the C trust did not exist monies over $600,000 that were not given outright to the survivor would be taxed. Most importantly, C trust money can compound in value if the tax on it is postponed until the death of the surviving spouse.

As a specific example, let us say that instead of having an estate of $1,200,000 we have an estate valuation of $1,600,000. Each spouse now represents $800,000 in assets. An A-B-C trust can be drafted in such a way that at the death of the first spouse half of the $1,600,000 is utilized, with $600,000 going into the B trust and $200,000 is placed into the C trust. Full advantage of the lifetime exemption can then be taken, with the additional $200,000 in the C trust which is not taxed until the survivor's death. The remaining $800,000 in A trust that never belonged to the first spouse continues to remain under the complete control of the second or surviving spouse. When the surviving spouse dies his or her estate is required to pay estate tax not only on the $200,000 of the original $800,000 that went into the A trust that was above the exemption limit, but the $200,000 that was placed into the C trust. In addition, no probate fees are required to be paid and the property can now pass to the children as beneficiaries named in the trust.

If you are a married person and if the value of the combined estate of you and your spouse can be expected to be greater than $1,200,000 on the date of death for both of you, then the Q-tip should be considered as part of your estate plan. It will give you and your spouse greater estate planning flexibility, control, and in addition will postpone paying estate taxes. The Q-tip can be especially advantageous for spouses who marry a second or a third time, and have children from a previous marriage. For example, if a women of means is a second or third spouse and not the mother of the testator's children, after her death she can employ a Q-tip to provide her current spouse with income during his life, while the trust assets are preserved for her children from a prior marriage after her current spouse dies.

Generation-Skipping Trust

People with larger estates can use a legal device—the generation skipping transfer—that will not only benefit their grandchildren but also minimize their estate tax burden. Prior to 1976, the grantor was permitted to provide a life estate in the form of income from a trust to his or her children. If only the income was collected by the children during their lifetime, then the principal could be transferred to the grandchildren at least two generations younger than the grantor, and the estate would escape some or all of any estate tax liability. This form of *direct skip* is now treated under current law and for federal estate tax purposes substantially the same as property interests that are transferred outright from one generation to a succeeding generation, and the tax is paid by the trust unless the will or trust provides otherwise. The trust can be created during the grantor's life as a living trust, or written into a will, in which case it will become a testamentary trust. If you create it in your will, the assets will have to pass through probate. Under current law, the skip tax is 55 percent and is paid, just as estate tax duties are required, at the time of the grantor's death. It is applied to assets given to the grandchildren through a trust arrangement or by direct transfer, but no transfer tax is due on the first million dollars to each person making generation-skipping transfers.* If you have a spouse, and the spouse agrees, you both can transfer to your grandchildren up to two million dollars tax free.

Trust arrangements involving generational skips require expert preparation and delicate wording that will not negate what you are attempting to solve. If you have decided to pass a million dollars to your grandchildren, and you know that *your* children will in some way benefit from the income and earnings that will be produced, then it might behoove you to consider a generation-skipping trust. Leaving money to your grandchildren when they are babies may be a premature act. For instance, your daughter-in-law divorces your son, receives custody of the children . . . . then moves out of the country, which makes it difficult for you to visit your grandchildren. If you had known this would happen would you have done it the same way? Perhaps a more prudent move would be to provide your children with more of your estate through an insurance trust and tax-free gifting by annual exclusion, or other distribution schemes under trust arrangements.

The greatest benefit of the generation-skipping trust is that taxes are saved on the transfer of assets. If you just leave your property directly to your children by will, the money will be taxed when you die and again when they die. Using this type of trust, one million dollars to each person skips one generation of estate taxes. The biggest negative, of course, is that *your* children will not receive any principal amount during their lifetime unless provisions are made to the contrary.

---

*There is a possibility that this amount may be indexed to inflation at some future time.

In the last two chapters trusts have been described in a very positive light. Although disadvantages were mentioned, all in all they appear to be excellent estate-planning tools. Taxes and public policy prevent the grantor from accomplishing everything he or she would like. Certainly, if they were the way for people to escape financial, legal and tax obligations, they wouldn't be available very long. But trusts do achieve significant estate tax savings for those who know how they are to be employed.

6

Grantor Trusts and the Family Limited Partnership

Almost anyone with some assets can benefit from the use of a trust. Trusts are very flexible instruments and can be designed and drafted for your particular estate-planning goals. You have to assess your needs, however, and those of your spouse and family as to what you would like to accomplish now and in the future. The planning choices discussed here fall into two categories: the grantor trust and the family limited partnership. Each, used properly, can be fundamental in providing tax-free property transfers and an income stream for you and your spouse.

Grantor Retained Income Trust (GRIT)

Although Congress has restricted its use, the Grantor Retained Income Trust, otherwise known by the acronym GRIT, can still be effective in estate planning and is particularly useful for single people who cannot make use of the marital deduction to reduce their estate tax liability. The GRIT is an irrevocable trust into which the grantor places property and retains the income and the use of the property for a period of years. After the specified term expires, the property in the trust can be held in further trust for the grantor's children or grandchildren, or distributed to them outright. But the grantor *must* survive the trust term. If he or she does, then the remainder interest, including all appreciation of its value, will pass to beneficiaries free from all estate taxes. If the grantor does not survive the term, the value of the remainder goes back into the grantor's estate and is taxed accordingly.

A GRIT permits you as grantor to transfer assets with reduced tax consequences while retaining the enjoyment and use of certain property for a specific period of time, usually not more than 10 years. It is basically a delayed gift set in motion currently but which will take effect at some later date. Because you can retain rights of value as the grantor, such as income from the trust property, the value of the gift at the end of the term of the trust for gift tax purposes is determined actuarially on the date of the transfer. A discounted valuation is justified because of the cost of waiting to receive this asset by someone in the future. Indeed, the longer the beneficiaries must wait for the receipt of property, the lower the gift tax value of the property and the lower the cost of the gift.

Who and what determines the value of this form of gift? It is computed with the help of actuarial valuation tables issued by the IRS and takes into account not only the property placed into the GRIT on the date of transfer, but also the term of the trust and the age of the grantor. In typical cases, gift tax liability can be less than half of what it would be if it were an outright gift. How much less or more would depend on, among other things, the discount rate used in the computations, which can fluctuate every month. If death occurs before the trust term expires, then the transferred trust property is returned to the grantor's estate and becomes subject to estate tax liability. The grantor, however, will receive a credit for any gift tax paid or a credit against the amount of the

$600,000 lifetime exemption equivalent used when the trust was funded. What would be irrevocably lost are the costs related to the formation of the trust and interest on any gift taxes paid.

Establishing a GRIT

What are *some* of the elements required in setting up a GRIT?

- An irrevocable trust must be established.
- The trust should be funded with income-producing property that is likely to increase in value.
- The trust document must provide that the grantor retains the right to enjoy trust income for a specific number of years.
- The trustee should be someone other than the grantor or the grantor's spouse.

Two important facts regarding the use of GRIT should be taken into account. As the grantor, you would be making a gift of the remainder, that is, the value of the property after the income interest is terminated. The gift will not make you qualify for the $10,000 annual exclusion because it is not a gift of present interest, which the beneficiary must be permitted to enjoy on a current basis and not have to wait for until the trust term ends. As a result, gift tax may have to be paid on the amount or be shielded by the use of part of your lifetime exemption equivalent. In addition, the beneficiary or beneficiaries will acquire your tax basis of the property transferred to the trust, and your estate would lose the option to use the stepped-up basis at your death. The big question is, Is it worth removing from the estate any appreciation of an asset placed into the trust for the trust term to reduce estate taxes as opposed to losing the use of the stepped-up tax basis that could be used without employing the GRIT? A comparison of these choices would have to be determined by an expert in this area.

The Revenue Reconciliation Act of 1990 disallowed GRIT from being funded with such securities as stocks, bonds, or partnership interests. It did, however, permit certain assets to be used, such as vacation homes, to a limited extent vacant land, paintings and other works of art, and, lastly, personal residences. From this comes the qualified personal residence trust, sometimes known as a residential GRIT.

Qualified Personal Residence Trust (QPRT)

Did you ever think that your home would offer you a unique estate-planning tax break? As a device for reducing taxes it has, at least at the time of this writing, survived the incursions and attacks by the Congress and the IRS, but for how long? It works like this. When a personal residence is placed into a GRIT it becomes a qualified personal residence trust (QPRT). It removes the value of your residence from your taxable estate while you continue to live in it during a specified term or until death. Essentially, this right can be considered the same as receiving income from the trust. It also allows members of the family to keep the family home after you die, instead of being forced to sell it in order to pay estate tax liability. But, in addition, because the residence is placed into the trust having a specific fair market value, any increase in valuation from that day until the time of the grantor's death is not included in the grantor's taxable estate even though it is likely to appreciate over the years during the term of the trust and beyond. A gift to the trust equal to the remainder interest in the property is subject to gift tax liability caused by the transfer, but the liability can be absorbed by using up a portion of one's lifetime exemption equivalent available. The precise values of the assets placed into the QPRT are computed from actuarial tables provided by the IRS and that have to do with the term of the trust, the grantor's age, and the value of the property.

The attraction of the QPRT is that you are able to get an asset out of your estate now that will be worth appreciably more after the term of years. This sounds good, but there are some disadvantages to consider.

1. Your beneficiaries will have to use *your* cost basis to determine what capital gain they will have to pay after you die and the house becomes theirs. The gain, in all likelihood, would be considerably less than what you would pay in estate taxes on the value of the house left in your estate without a trust and, in addition, having to pay probate costs.

2. You can become a tenant at sufferance, which means a tenancy that holds over beyond the term of the agreement. Even though after the income term expires, and you as grantor lose the legal right to the house, arrangements can be made to lease it at fair market rental rates so that you, and if circumstances dictate your spouse, may live in the house and pay rent to the trust and beneficiaries. If this is decided upon, be sure not to do it at the same time the trust is established. Wait for some later date so you won't take a chance on losing your tax advantage by a reversion of ownership out of the trust and into your estate.

3. If you pass away during the agreed to term, the entire value of your home is brought back into your taxable estate.

4. While you remain in the house you continue to pay

the usual expenses of the house, including property taxes, which you can deduct on your federal tax return.

If you would like to sell the house during the term of the trust agreements, it can be done. But the trust must reinvest or terminate and distribute the funds from the sale to the grantor or link the QPRT to a grantor retained annuity trust (GRAT), which will be discussed later. The grantor and the trust are considered by the IRS to be one taxpayer, and as grantor you will have to pay any capital gains tax when the house is sold.

You are also permitted to employ the "over 55" one-time, $125,000 lifetime capital gains exclusion on the sale of a principal residence to reduce any taxes. The trustee must still reinvest the funds within two years after the sale or convert to a GRAT. The grantor also has the choice of paying the tax from his or her personal assets not in the trust, or withdraw the amount of the tax from the trust. From a tax standpoint, the former is more desirable because the trust assets are not reduced and the grantor can remove additional monies from his or her estate.

The most attractive element of a residential GRIT is that it permits you to make use of all or part of the current lifetime exemption equivalent that can pass gift and estate tax free to your beneficiaries. Leveraging of the credit comes into play by the fact that the gift tax, if any, is based on the present value of the remainder interest of the gift to the donee and is discounted by the cost of waiting, the grantor's right to occupy the home and the risks involved in having the property revert to the grantor's estate if he or she dies during the term of the GRIT.

The GRAT and the GRUT

Except for the personal resident trust, just discussed, the 1990 Revenue Act substantially reduced the effectiveness of the GRIT as an estate-planning device. But two other planning tools have been introduced somewhat similar to the GRIT. They are known as the grantor retained annuity trust (GRAT) and the grantor retained unitrust (GRUT). The grantor can create either one of them by transferring property to the trust and retaining a qualified annuity or unitrust interest in the property. Either is treated as the grantor having made an irrevocable gift to the remainderman of the remainder interest in the property. The trust lasts for a specified period and the trust property passes to the heirs who are members of the grantor's family. The grantor, however, must outlive the trust term in order for the property to pass without tax liability. If this does not occur the amount reverts to the grantor's estate.

Income that the grantor receives from these grantor trusts is not necessarily all of the income that the trust makes from its investments. The GRAT is required to have a payout of a specific *fixed dollar amount.* On the other hand, the GRUT pays the grantor a specific *percentage* of the value of the trust computed on an annual basis. In addition, great care must be taken in establishing payout schedules, especially for the GRAT. Because the GRAT pays a constant dollar amount to the grantor irrespective of any capital appreciation or gains, its mandatory payment schedule might require the sale of assets if not enough income is generated by the investments in the trust portfolio.

To be useful as estate-planning devices, a GRAT and a GRUT depend to a large measure on the rate of return that the trust receives from its investments. If the returns are greater than the assumed U.S. Treasury interest rate tables indicate,* then the excess is accumulated in the trust and outside the grantor's taxable estate. The assumed rate is established on a monthly basis, and if asset

---

*All annuity interests are valued under section 7520 of the U.S. tax code.

values are projected at a rate equal to what the assumptions are, the value of the remainder interest will be correct. If they grow at a lesser rate the remainder interest would have been overvalued at the time the trust was created. Hence, the gift tax paid or the unified credit used would have been too high compared with the total value of the property contributed to the trust. An adjustment would have to be made. If the opposite occurred and the rate of return received to the trust is higher than the assumed rate, then the increased value of the assets is transferred to the beneficiaries free of transfer tax. So you see, the GRAT can be especially effective if funded with higher yielding corporate bonds, mutual bond funds, or other high income-producing investments when the assumed IRS rate is lower.

If, in your planning considerations, you believe that this type of grantor trust might be useful to you, you will need to (1) arrive at a trust payout schedule for yourself as grantor, (2) decide whether or not you should chose a GRAT or a GRUT, (3) determine the amount of the grantor's retained annuity or unitrust interests, and (4) do all the calculations required to obtain actuarial values and the remainder interest(s).

Because GRIT can no longer be funded with such assets as stocks, mutual funds, bonds, etc., GRAT and GRUT have now, to a large extent, replaced the GRIT in employing financial assets as part of trust property. Using them, however, does not give you the leveraging characteristics, nor are they as effective as, say, a personal residence GRIT, just discussed. But they are another way to transfer financial assets and other property to members of the grantor's family at reduced transfer costs. The rules are very complicated, and, if not understood and followed, any possible tax break could be lost.

Despite limitations placed on grantor trusts, such trusts should continue to be an effective estate-planning tool for the transfer of property to family at a reduced tax cost. The documents, however, must be crafted and drawn by a very experienced estate planning expert. The rules and regulations are stringent and unyielding. If you choose to create a grantor trust, be aware of the fact that the IRS and Congress may, sometime in the future, impose additional requirements that might apply to any trust you have that is already in existence. Accordingly, it would be prudent to give the trustee the powers to qualify the trust by the use of amendments and other additional changes that may be required in the future. So state in your trust agreement that the trust *intends to qualify* so that you will be sure that it will later meet all new requirements. The grantor's intent to do this is not enough.

Another factor that deserves consideration is that the GRAT and the GRUT can only achieve tax avoidance if the grantor survives the term of the retained interest. If he or she does not, then the property is returned to the grantor's taxable estate. Additionally, you, as grantor, should also be aware of the fact that if you survive and live for any significant length of time after the term ends, no income will be available to you from the property because it passes to the remainderman. It may be prudent, therefore, to make doubly certain that you will have *enough other assets* to produce a stream of income to fulfill your and your spouse's financial needs.

Family Limited Partnership

A family limited partnership (FLP) is a type of estate-planning tool that allows you to retain control over assets that you give away to other family members; its desirable tax benefits can be advantageous to you. Properly planned and executed, it is a very attractive option for your estate income and tax planning.

Typically, an FLP is created by a father, mother, or both under your state's laws on partnership and must have a general partner and at least one limited partner. One parent generally retains the role of the general partner and makes the managerial and financial decisions while the limited partners are not permitted to have any role at all in management. The point here is to allow the general partner to transfer, over a period of time, general partnership property interests and any income that can be attributed to those interests to younger family members while leveraging the unified credit or the gift tax annual exclusion. The assets that are transferred to the partnership by the donor parents can be securities, such as stocks, bonds, mutual funds, or real estate, among other assets. For example, shares of General Electric stock can be gifted to other generation family members as limited partners at current market value without gift tax consequences. In addition, any appreciation in the value of the shares within the partnership are removed from the donor's personal taxable estate, thereby escaping subsequent tax liability. Another useful element of the FLP is that it can be employed to protect partnership assets from potential creditors of the partners.

But, with little doubt, the main incentive for hiring an attorney and spending the money required in establishing an FLP is the significant leveraging available through valuation discounts. Essentially, the gift tax value of the asset is usually much less than the fair market value because there is no "willing buyer" and "willing seller" approach as you would have in any open market. In addition to this lack of marketability, partnership assets owned by a minority interest, generally don't allow for the withdrawal of those minority-owned interests. For example, if you as a general partner transferred certain assets to your son, whose partnership representation is limited and whose minority partnership restrictions do not allow his participation in the business, what is your son's limited interest worth? Certainly not "market value." His ownership value must be discounted. The range of discounts permitted would depend to a great extent on the type of asset that is involved, but the discounts could indeed range from 20–50 percent and are specifically recognized and sanctioned by the IRS.

There is little doubt that the transfer of discounted interests to your younger family members that can later on have substantial value is a way to provide significant generational wealth shifting. The FLP should, however, be taken advantage of *currently* because this excellent estate planning tool may not be permitted to last forever.

Further, a limited family partnership arrangement can be placed in trust for the benefit of family members rather than the donor making outright gift(s) to other family members. But ownership of assets must then be vested in the trustee, who should be unrelated and independent of the grantor-donor. Indeed, the FLP, if it is crafted by an experienced attorney, can serve as a cornerstone of your family gift planning. In addition to providing tax advantages, it has become popular in the 1990s for its simplicity of organization, limited liability, valuation discounts, and creditor protection.

Essentially, this chapter on grantor trusts describes their use and how the transferor-grantor is allowed to create a trust reserving the income from the trust for a period of years. At the end of the trust term the property passes to members of the transferor's family who are in a lower (younger) generation, such as children and grandchildren. But its main purpose for you the grantor is to leverage your unified credit.

The personal residence trust can also be employed as an estate-planning device if you enjoy harmonious rela-

tionships with members of the family and intended beneficiaries. It allows you to transfer your home out of your
taxable estate and to your chosen beneficiaries at a reduced transfer tax value. You should remember, however, that when you have retained property rights or an
income interest yourself, the asset does not receive a
"stepped up" tax basis at the death of the grantor. The
basis is what you paid for it, and your heirs would have
to pay the capital gains tax on the appreciated property.

7

The Advantages of
Charitable Gifting

Understanding and applying estate planning techniques
and strategies, as we have learned, can be beneficial in
many ways to you and your family. But, up to this point,
we have not mentioned an important part of the subject,
and one that is employed by many people. It is charitable
giving. Each year, in deciding on the final distribution
and disposition of their estate, many astute planners designate a certain portion of their assets that have been accumulated over the years, for the support and benefit of
one or several of America's charitable organizations. Gifting, indeed, has become a tradition in this country, especially when, for some reason, it could not have taken
place earlier in the donor's life. Although there is the
high moral purpose and satisfaction that you can receive
for your gift giving, a more compelling reason may exist
for many. Whenever you donate money or property to a
charity, you as a donor, not only receive current income
tax benefits but you will also lower your death taxes by
shrinking the value of your estate. Indeed, any gift made
to a charity that has received tax-exempt status from the
Internal Revenue Service, does not require the donor to
pay federal estate taxes provided the organization receiving the gift is qualified to receive the exemption. Qual-

ified organizations described under IRS code section 501(c)(3) can be nonprofit educational and medical research institutions, nonprofit hospitals, private operating foundations, public charities, federal, state, and local governments, and any organization operated solely for religious purposes. In addition, if you pay an expense that a charity has incurred, it also can qualify as a deduction. Examples of deductions that do not qualify would include those contributions made to your chambers of commerce, political parties, social clubs, and business and civic leagues. In order for a contribution to be deductible it is required to be made by check, cash, or credit card. If it is personal property it must be delivered to the charity and receipted. If it is real property, a legal transfer must have taken place in order for the deduction to be valid.

When you decide to do your income tax return for the year, you should know that charitable gifts of cash or property are fully deductible but are limited to a percentage of your adjusted gross income (AGI), and this percentage is dependent on the type of charity receiving the gift. For instance, a deductible contribution to qualified charities and churches may not exceed 50 percent of your AGI under current law. A contribution to a veterans or fraternal organization, on the other hand, is permitted only a 30 percent limitation on deductions of AGI. If the amount of the write-off is more than 50 percent of the donor's AGI, then the excess amount can be carried forward for up to five additional years until used up.

Let's say that the gift you intend to make happens to be shares of stock, a mutual fund, or some bonds that you have held for years. The asset has depreciated in value from the time you purchased it. Would it be wise to donate the security under these circumstances? Probably not. You should try to time your donation so you will be able to take advantage of any capital loss. You won't be permitted to do this by making a gift at fair market value to the charity. You should sell the security first, take the loss, apply it against any capital gains you have and then donate the proceeds or a part thereof to charity.

Clearly, if you are one of the many people who are motivated to benefit an educational institution, a fraternal organization, or even your own government, and if your estate would otherwise be subject to a significant estate tax, charitable gifting may be an estate-planning option for you to consider. As a donor, you will reduce the cost of your charitable gift and allow yourself to give more than perhaps you would have given if no tax savings were made available.

With this in mind, deriving benefits from planned giving arrangements can be accomplished in many forms. You can donate property by will, by bequest, and as discussed later, under a charitable trust arrangement. If it is done by will, for instance, it will afford you the opportunity to (1) direct how and to whom the property is to be distributed, (2) specify when such distributions are to be made, (3) select a guardian to take care of any minor children, and (4) choose a financial institution or individual(s) you wish to carry out your wishes.

The *charitable bequest* will designate a portion of your assets to be used to benefit a charity or several charities. Bequests can take different forms. Some are *general*, and others very *specific*. The latter type is a popular way of leaving a more detailed or limited dollar amount or a particular piece of real or personal property.

Charitable Trusts

You may recall that trusts are broadly described as living or testamentary, revocable or irrevocable. The basic form of a charitable trust can be either living, that is, created during your lifetime, or testamentary, established in your will and which takes effect at your death. Tax benefits can be considerable, but the trust, if created as a living trust, must be irrevocable in order for the tax benefits to be received. Your tax deduction is usually based on the current fair market value of the contributed asset. In addition, you as donor can indicate how the specific charity is to use the money after you have passed away. Charitable trusts, by the way, can last indefinitely. The rule against perpetuities, which restricts the use of other trusts to a life in being plus twenty-one years, does not apply to charitable trusts.

Because of increases in the income tax rate for individuals that came into law in 1993, it is less expensive for prospective donors to make gifts to one of the many qualified charitable organizations than it was before 1993. When your tax bracket increases, your out-of-pocket costs for gifting fall. Although higher tax rates tend to discourage investment, they are apt to foster and even encourage tax-deductible activities. In addition, prior to 1993, certain donors of charitable gifts, who were then subject to the alternative minimum tax* (AMT), were not permitted to deduct from taxes the current fair market value of their charitable gift and instead could only deduct what was the original cost basis. If, for instance, you paid $10,000 for a painting and it is now worth $50,000, you can now qualify for a tax deduction on the current appraised value and no tax is required to be paid on the $40,000 capital gain. The donor, however, may deduct the contribution only in the year that the gift is actually made.

----

*The alternative minimum tax (AMT) operates by establishing a separate tax calculation parallel to the regular federal income tax computation. If it exceeds your regular tax, the excess is added to your current bill. AMT is generally levied against individuals with large amounts of income who wish to take advantage of otherwise allowable deductions and credits for the purpose of reducing tax liability.

Charitable Remainder Trust

A remainder trust permits you or another named person or persons, to receive income from trust assets until you or your income beneficiaries die. The remaining trust assets are then donated to the charity you choose, free of federal estate or income tax liability. As an estate-planning device, the charitable remainder trust can be drafted slightly differently for each set of circumstances, but in general it attempts to accomplish one thing: for you to take highly appreciated assets that you might have owned for years, have them donated to a charity, and receive substantial tax benefits. Prime candidates for assets would, for instance, be investment securities, such as stocks and bonds, and long-held acreage or other real estate having increased in value over the years and having unrealized capital gains. Would you, for example, sell assets in your name, take the gain, pay the taxes, and *then* make the charitable contribution? Absolutely not! These assets should be sold by the charity tax-free to you and replaced by other assets offering higher returns. The purpose of this property transfer is to convert a low yielding asset mix to a high and steady income stream for you, your spouse, and children perhaps, during your lifetime and theirs.

When the assets are accepted by an IRS qualified charity, you are permitted to receive an immediate write-off equal to the discounted present value of the gift. IRS valuation tables will then help you or your adviser calculate the amount you can legally deduct from your income tax. The extent of the write-off also depends upon the age of the beneficiaries. It is smaller if younger persons are the income recipients because younger persons have longer to live statistically and consequently will receive more payments than an older person. Because of this, a smaller remainder amount will be available to the charity, consequently, the smaller write-off. Income that is accumulated in the charity's account from investments is not taxable to the charity. Income, however, that is received by you or any other beneficiaries is fully taxable in the year that it is received.

You should keep in mind that in creating a remainder trust your decision will not be able to be changed at some time in the future. It is irrevocable and once established as a living trust during your lifetime or as a testamentary trust by will, the terms cannot be altered. But you will, however, be able to change trustees and charitable beneficiaries if you wish. An independent trustee can be used, although you can choose to be your own trustee or to have the charity you named as beneficiary manage the assets. The trustee, however, will have to be given not only authority over the investment management of the trust but other discretionary powers as well. The amount of income that you will receive periodically from the transferred assets is directly related to the success of the trustee in managing the assets of the trust.

Charitable Annuity and Unitrusts

There are two other remainder trusts that are worth mentioning: the charitable remainder annuity trust and unitrust. The *Annuity Trust* is established by making a one-time contribution of principal; it requires a distribution of a minimum of 5 percent of the initial fair market value of the assets at the time the trust is established, and once every year thereafter. The percentage of pay out of the initial fair market value remains fixed and you are not permitted to add assets to this type of trust. Treasury regulations and annuity tables control the amount of the current tax deduction to which you, as donor, are entitled. This deduction is based on the present value of this future gift to charity, the age of the donor, the rate of interest computed to determine benefits that the beneficiaries will receive, and the amount of earnings paid out. At the death of the grantor, the remainder interest, which depends upon how long the grantor-donor lives and the earnings from trust assets, is transferred to the named charity.

The charitable remainder *Unitrust* also requires the placing of assets into the trust, especially those that have appreciated over the years. The trust, on the other hand, must distribute at least 5 percent of the market value of the trust assets on an annual basis. The amount of the distributions are revalued annually, consequently the amount that the income beneficiaries receive fluctuates somewhat depending on how well or how poorly the investments in the trust perform. If the income received by beneficiaries from the trust investments falls below the 5 percent benchmark level (not including capital gains), only income need be distributed. This differs from the annuity trust in which a fixed percentage of the initial market value is disbursed.

Another difference between the two is that the unitrust allows for a catch-up provision, giving the donor an opportunity to make additional payments into the trust when less than 5 percent was paid to the income beneficiaries, usually the husband and wife. The gift that the donor makes to the unitrust is considered final when the trust is established. At that time, you, as donor, receive an immediate tax deduction that is based on your age, the discount rate, the amount of income the beneficiary(ies) will receive, and the amount of the gift. Any income that is received by you from assets invested by the charity is your sole responsibility and income tax must be paid on the amount you receive each year. Income that is not distributed accumulates in the trust tax-free. Any profits or capital gains made by the trust because of the sale of assets is not taxable to you.

Let's take an illustration of how a typical unitrust works and what the tax benefits are to you as donor. You are 65 years old and a graduate of a well-known university, and you wish to make a charitable gift to your school by establishing a charitable remainder unitrust that will pay you income for life and provide you with tax benefits as well. Your portfolio shows appreciated securities now worth $100,000 that were purchased many years ago for a total cost of $20,000.

Principal to trust	$100,000
Income tax deduction at age 65. Amount of deduction will vary somewhat with the age of the donor and the IRS discount rate	$ 49,000±
Savings on income tax = 49,000 × 36 percent rate	$ 17,600±
Tax savings on capital gain: $100,000–$20,000 (cost basis) = $80,000. 80,000 × 28 percent	$ 22,400±
Income to beneficiary after first year which will increase each year based on total return received and added to principal.	$ 5,000

Figure 7.1   Tax Benefits to Unitrust Donors

A disadvantage of the unitrust stems from the costs involved in administering the asset revaluation process each year. Although perhaps small in amount, over time it can retain a somewhat diminished remainder interest for the charity. But the remainder trust concept continues to be popular, especially for the donor who does not have close relatives or does not wish to leave any assets to members of the family. For the family members, however, who might have counted on the money, it no doubt would be a disappointment even though they may recognize that the money is going to a worthy cause.

Charitable Gift Annuity

One of the simplest and perhaps oldest methods of establishing a tax-saving annuity is by means of a charitable gift annuity. It is a combination of an investment and a gift in which marketable securities and/or cash is transferred to a charity that will guarantee by contract to pay to the donor and beneficiary a specified annuity. It can be set up as an *immediate annuity* or one that is deferred. The donor is permitted to claim a current tax deduction on the portion of the transferred cash/securities that represents the charitable gift element, which is the amount by which the value of the property transferred to the charity exceeds the value of the annuity received. A portion of each annuity payment is treated as a return of capital and is received income tax-free over the life expectancy of the annuitant-beneficiary.

Deferred-Payment Gift Annuity

Somewhat different, but an extension of the annuity concept just discussed, is the deferred-payment annuity that may have greater appeal to a somewhat younger donor with very high current income. If you are about 45 or 50 years old and would like a tax deduction now, for retirement income later, you might consider this type of income annuity program. You will receive the immediate charitable deduction for the gift portion of each transfer of marketable securities, cash, real or personal property to a deferred payment-gift annuity. Contributions to the plan can be made on a periodic basis over the years as a single transfer or a series of transfers. In return, the charitable organization agrees to pay you, the donor, and/or your spouse, annuity income starting at some future date, generally about the time of retirement. A part of each annuity payment will be a tax-free return of principal and paid out proportionally over the donor's life expectancy or over the life expectancy of both spouses.

Pooled-Interest Trusts

Pooled-interest trusts are also known as pooled-income trusts. As the name suggests, your gift, and gifts by others, are placed in investment pools so that the best rates of return can be received by the charity. It is especially useful to those donors who prefer making smaller contributions of cash or marketable securities to the charity over a period of time, rather than a lump-sum contribution. Pooled trusts are irrevocable and are maintained and managed by the particular charitable institution that divides the income proportionately among the various contributors. The donor, or his or her designated beneficiary, receives a life interest in the income stream produced by the fund, and each donor's participation is based on the amount of units held in exchange for assets contributed and overall earnings of the charity. It is highly likely that contemplated gifts contributed to a pooled trust are usually less than $50,000 to $75,000 and the trust pays for the drafting of the documents and whatever fees may be charged by a trustee. If the gift is more than the above amount, it may be more appropriate to have your attorney design and draft a charitable remainder trust that can give you more flexibility and perhaps

greater income. At the death of the last income beneficiary, the charity acquires title to all of the property interests that you have had, including those that remain in the
pooled trust.

Charitable Lead Trust

Charitable lead trusts, also known as charitable income
trusts, are usually testamentary in nature and involve
your transfer of property into a trust that is directed to
pay income to the charity of your choice. As compared
to the remainder trusts just discussed, the dispositions
are reversed. The charity receives the periodic stream of
income rather than you. After a lead trust is created and
the donated property is placed in the trust, if the investments currently held are not income-oriented securities,
the holdings are sold tax-free to the donor and new securities having higher rates of return are placed in the trust
to create a greater income stream for the charity. These
income distributions are received by the trust for a set
number of years. After the agreed-to, predetermined period ends, the principal reverts to you, your family, or
to beneficiaries or whomever the creator of the trust had
named originally.

What, in fact, has been created by this income trust is
an *income* interest that the grantor has donated to a charity while retaining the future *ownership* interest for the
designated beneficiaries. Current law is designed to reduce the amount of deduction claimed for the current
value of trust income payable to a charity. In certain limited situations the charity's income interest can be
claimed, but the valuation requires a complex set of evaluations. Generally speaking, however, the longer the
trust term and the higher the payments, the greater the
deduction you will receive. The opposite is also true.

This limitation on the deductibility of trust income and the fact the assets placed into the trust are subject to estate taxes when you die mean that the lead trust has become a less desirable estate-planning tool than the previously discussed remainder trust. It may, however, be considered a little more seriously as a tax-planning option if you and your family have less need for current income.

For many years the federal tax code has been a good friend to charitable organizations. It has permitted the deductibility of contributions, which in large measure is responsible for the fact that Americans give so generously. But not everyone has the desire to benefit a charity with a gift. If you do, but you are concerned about reducing the inheritance to your children and the possible hurt it might promote, you can solve the problem by establishing another trust, having it purchase an insurance policy on your life, and making the required periodic premium payments. In this way, your children and perhaps others you wish to name as beneficiaries would receive an amount essentially equal to the size of the charitable gift. The question of hurt feelings would then be resolved.

Before you make any transfers to a charity or charitable trust, there are several points to consider. After you have contacted the charity of your choice,

1. Make sure it is recognized by the IRS as a charity.
2. Speak with the coordinator of planned-giving programs.
3. Decide which of your assets you wish to donate to the charity. Which would be the most appropriate? Should it be done under a trust arrangement and, if so, under what circumstances?
4. Determine who pays for creating the charitable trust, whether it is you, the charity, or both of you.

The charity may have the proper forms but they must be scrutinized.

5. Decide in what manner the income is to be received: monthly, semiannually or annually, etc.
6. Have your accountant determine the actual write-off that you will receive.

If you are the kind of person who wishes to benefit your school, church, or other favorite charity with a major gift, not only will you receive tax benefits and a degree of personal satisfaction for you and your family, but some public recognition as well. Charitable gifting, however, is only one aspect of your mission. The other is to protect and manage your estate and pass it on in time, as best you can to future generations. You can lay the cornerstone to your estate planning by carefully employing some of the suggestions proposed in this chapter, especially using a remainder trust that names members of your family or you and your spouse as partial beneficiaries of the trust, as opposed to giving up all the property irrevocably at the time of the gift. While it is probably true that the tax consequences can be very attractive for an outright gift, many people find it difficult to do. The remainder trust is a good compromise. It can allow you, as donor, to receive a current tax deduction by donating highly appreciated property to a remainder trust with no capital gains liability and also may provide an income stream for life from the trust's investments for you and your spouse. In addition, your estate taxes and probate costs are later reduced because the value of the gift you made is removed from your estate. It is without a doubt a very effective estate-planning tool.

Any tax-saving, planned-giving program can be an appropriate and helpful way for you to contribute to your favorite charitable organization. You can not only attain your philanthropic goals but also fill specific public needs to benefit society as a whole. Our tax laws recognize charitable giving and provide incentives and encouragement to you and other prospective donors to minimize your after-tax cost of contributions and maximize the tax benefits to you that current law allows. Shouldn't charitable giving, then, be a consideration as part of your planning in developing a tax-saving estate program?

8

Mutual Fund Investment Management

Most of the discussion so far has dealt with the legal and tax implications of estate planning and your ability to transfer wealth from one generation to another. But there is another part of estate planning that is just as important. In its broader aspect, estate planning also concerns itself with the increase and preservation of wealth during your life and for sometime after. This is what we can broadly call premortem and postmortem investment planning. It has to do with designing and maintaining a long-term investment program with realistic objectives to provide a certain degree of financial security for you, your family, and possible beneficiaries.

There are several ways in which the responsibility for conserving and increasing wealth falls upon you while you are still active. You can be your own investor, a trustee, a cotrustee, an executor, or you can be given authority to manage a portfolio of securities by someone else in the form of a trading authorization from a mutual fund management company or stock brokerage firm. This authority can be limited, or it can be given without restrictions as to what type of securities to invest in. Regardless of what particular role you play currently, perhaps as a generalist overseeing your assets, as a fiduciary managing a trust, or as an investor making specific investment decisions, you probably will need someone else to manage your assets when you choose not to do it anymore or for some reason, you cannot. This chapter, therefore, covers the use of professional money management through mutual fund investing and the administration and supervision of assets by other means.

Risk and Return

Investing is easy to do. Investing successfully for yourself over a period of years is not so easy. There are so many imponderables in the market: economic, social, emotional, and psychological factors at work, as well as market forces themselves in the form of demand and supply factors. Because of these variables, being consistently right most of the time is difficult. A great effort must be devoted to the securities markets and to particular areas of investment in order to become and stay successful. As an investor for your own account, or one making decisions in the role of a trustee or cotrustee, your investment choices can be critical to the ultimate success of the program. Others are interested in your success also. Don't be surprised to find your beneficiaries looking over your shoulder to see how you are managing "their" money.

Risk in investment planning, and the assumption of a particular level of risk, is critical in determining the type and allocation of securities within a managed portfolio. Measuring this risk beforehand as best you can and matching it with the financial goals you subscribe to is fundamental in establishing appropriate investment practices. If the risk factors appear to be inordinately high, then an adjustment is required. Although you may think that you possess the necessary acumen to be a consistently successful investor while you are active, a long-term plan to promote and sustain your financial objectives can be attained into the future more easily by a professional who is representative of your thinking and goals. An investment program needs to be well balanced with growth-oriented securities as well as a fixed-income component to give your portfolio stability and a revenue stream. An increase of your asset base of between 12–15 percent per year is quite possible by utilizing the concept of *total return*, which simply means the receipt of dividends and/or interest plus capital gains or losses.

Investment Guidelines and Strategy

From the perspective of an estate-planning investor, it would be wise not to do any investing until you have decided on those objectives and investment goals that appear to be the right choice for you and your family. Guidelines for investing should be correlated with and adapted to your particular financial situation and circumstance. For instance, how will your choice of investment strategy effect your current lifestyle and how might it eventually impact your spouse and the beneficiaries of your estate? The investment strategy discussed here is not an attempt to strictly categorize investments by age bracket, which would misrepresent the goal-setting theories so important in investing. One criterion in determining what is an appropriate investment is the ability to accept the conventional wisdom of an increasing and decreasing level of risk attributable to certain types of securities. Obviously few people would risk their life savings to buy shares of a highly speculative new company when they know they can lose everything if it doesn't work out. As a young person working full time, you might take the chance, but at a later age with a spouse and children to take care of, you are less likely to. Therefore, if you or the person or persons for whom you are investing are about fifty years old, your investment strategy should be somewhat more conservative than for a younger person and lend greater weight to the concept of total return rather than a program of aggressive capital growth having a higher degree of risk. Retirement planning also needs to be considered in your investment mix. This, in all probability, would require a certain percentage of your available funds to be placed into tax-deferred investments so there is an accumulation of assets not hampered by the payment of taxes. If this has not already been accomplished, it might be wise to start such a program now, combined with your overall estate planning.

If your investing involves you or a trust for other persons in the 60 years and older age group, then you would need to increase your income strategy somewhat and eliminate any risky investment components in your portfolio. No one, however, has felt the impact of even a modest inflation more than those who are on a reduced work schedule and who rely on fixed-incomes. A small percentage of this portfolio, therefore, should still emphasize capital gains strategies and should involve the purchase of shares in companies with high visibility growth and uptrending earnings patterns.

Asset Allocation and Management

An asset allocation approach toward investing is basically a method of diversification employed by professionals to create an appropriate investment portfolio balance with enough flexibility to shift the allocation when there is reason to believe a change in emphasis is required. A shift can, for instance, take place because of an estimation of overvaluation or undervaluation of securities in the portfolio, financial or economic changes, or for strictly fundamental reasons, such as a loss in the pattern of earnings momentum, to name a few. Asset allocation takes in the idea of risk and return, safety and flexibility. It requires you to develop investment strategies that are expressed in terms of percentages of the total value of your portfolio of securities and what types of investments it contains at a particular time. For example, what percentage of your portfolio is invested in growth stocks, in government securities, in municipal bonds, and what specifically is not included and why. Asset allocation can be an extension of your personal investment philosophy and attempts to measure your strategy by allocation of securities having differing risks and differing growth and income patterns. Although diversification can provide protection in changing market investments, risks still prevail. There is no single asset allocation model that will protect your investments all of the time in all types of economic and market environments. Asset allocation requires time and a diligent and systematic review of individual and collective investments in a portfolio.

As an investor for your own account you have the freedom to allocate investment money in any manner you wish. If, however, you accept appointment as a trustee, you are under a legal obligation to act as a fiduciary and to invest in such a prudent manner as to protect and to administer the assets of the trust based on what is described in the trust document. In addition, you are required to achieve an acceptable rate of return on investments, that is, making the trust property productive for your income beneficiaries. But do you really want to accept that responsibility and challenge? Individual investing, that is making decisions and providing constant oversight as to what securities to buy, when to hold and when to sell, requires a great deal of time, knowledge, and the temperament and willingness to do the continuing research required for possible success in the marketplace. Is it not more prudent to take advantage of what a mutual fund or trust company can offer? By using professional management you will be able to duplicate to a large extent the same type of strategy and security selection that you might invest in individually and essentially match the low risk plan of action that you yourself would employ. As you get older, you will appreciate the reduced amount of bookkeeping that is required, as opposed to what is necessary to keep records for individual purchases and sales of securities and tax reporting. It is also less expensive if you use a no-load group of funds. I am a strong advocate of the no-load mutual fund concept for estate-planning investments and would like to describe here how mutual funds work.

Mutual Funds

A mutual fund can be many things to many people: an investment company, a diversified portfolio of securities, or an investment pool of money. Clearly, it is all of those things. It promises the professional money management required to invest in today's global, very complex, volatile and fast moving securities markets. Through diversification, asset allocation strategies, and oversight and review, mutual funds provide investors with a margin of safety that is usually available only to those who have substantial amounts of money to invest.

From a purely technical standpoint a mutual fund is an *open-end* investment company that can issue and sell shares continuously without any provision for a fixed capitalization, and must redeem the shares on demand. An investor can choose from hundreds of mutual funds, and sometimes it is not so easy to make the right choice. But if you know your stated investment objectives, you should have some idea what type of stocks, bonds, or other securities the portfolio manager is investing in by checking its latest annual report. The share price is recalculated every day based on how much or how little the underlying shares (that is the actual companies whose shares the mutual fund holds) fluctuate.

Risk factors associated with mutual fund shares are directly related to the investments that are made by its management company. If, for example, the underlying securities are corporate bonds and preferred stocks, it is probably an income-oriented fund and theoretically less risky than owning shares of a common stock fund. I say "theoretically" because in periods of increasing interest rates, interest-rate-sensitive preferred stocks, bonds, etc., will go down in price so their yield can meet the level of interest rates in the country in like securities. As a consequence, mutual-fund risk factors depend on not only what securities are in the portfolio of the fund but how those securities react to daily market and economic conditions. This, in turn, will be reflected in the *net asset value* (NAV) of the fund. The net asset value of a fund is calculated by taking the value of all of its investments plus the cash that it holds, subtracting fund expenses, and then dividing that amount by the number of currently outstanding shares in the fund. The result is the value of a single share or net asset value per share. A mutual fund gives you on-going professional management that you pay for through a sales charge, or a load, *and* management fee. Many funds do not charge a load. Investing by purchasing mutual fund shares is a relatively inexpensive way to invest, and if you select the right fund, your investment will grow in value over the years. Selection, of course, is the key and research will open the door.

Essentially, most mutual funds rely on diversification, and therefore market-risk factors are reduced as compared to buying shares of individual companies while managing your own portfolio of specific stocks. Funds generally have a broad asset allocation of securities, and the management of a stock fund, for example, does not usually allocate more than 25 percent of its total assets in securities of companies in a single industry but covers various types of industries. You can determine exactly what the fund's allocation of securities is and what else they do with your investment money if you send for its prospectus and the latest financial report.

Mutual funds have differing investment objectives and are classified into the following groups:

Growth or Common Stock Funds
Growth and Income Funds
Balanced Funds
Income or Bonds Funds
Convertible Bond Funds
U.S. Government Securities Funds
Tax-free Funds
Index Funds

Growth or Common Stock Funds

Growth or common stock funds actively seek with slight variation in degree to achieve primarily long-term growth of capital by means of realizing capital gains. Although no single definition can describe all funds that fall in this growth or common stock funds category, most offer comparatively low yields and have higher risks than the other types of mutual funds that will be mentioned. Owning a growth or stock mutual fund has, in general, been a very rewarding investment in the last decade, because the demand for growth stocks has persisted regardless of the inherent market risks involved.

Growth and Income Funds

The purpose of growth and income funds is to provide current income and long-term growth of capital. They attempt to do this by holding the greater percentage of their assets in common stocks and the rest in government securities and high-yielding preferred stocks and bonds. The basic difference between a growth-oriented stock fund and a growth and income fund is really a matter of degree. The emphasis in the latter is on a little less risk and more income. Growth and income mutual funds can fall into our investment philosophy providing their underlying shares do not appear to have high risks. Validating this can be done to some extent by checking the allocation of the securities within their portfolio. Make sure that the fund doesn't have more than 60 percent of its portfolio in common stock, and that stocks should be in the high yield category.

Balanced Funds

Balanced funds attempt to achieve long-term growth of principal without incurring a high degree of risk. They ordinarily keep in their portfolios a certain specified proportion of fixed-income securities and preferred stock, generally about 55 to 65 percent, as well as a lesser amount of common stock. As a result, these funds don't show as large a gain in net asset value during rising markets as you would find in common stock growth funds, but, by the same token, the funds net asset value will suffer less of a financial setback in markets that are declining. Because balanced funds allocate almost half of their portfolio toward income but also look for minimal capital gains, they more than any other group of mutual funds fit into the total-return objectives. It is a way of diversifying within the same fund.

There are many balanced funds, and the managers of these funds can have a somewhat different outlook on the allocation of securities and slightly different approach toward investment risk, but most of the funds fit into the general category of risk-averse, somewhat conservative, and middle of the road. When the overall market is volatile, a fairly steady balance is kept between various types of securities, some of which tend to fluctuate more in price and others hardly at all. It would be up to you to decide what balance you are comfortable with: whether common stocks should comprise 60 percent of the portfolio or 35–40 percent or whether fixed-income securities should be 75 percent of the total portfolio. The prospectus and annual report will give you the current allocations and then you can make the decision. In my opinion, an even balance between the two is a good choice to protect you from sharp swings in the stock market, and a fixed-income component to give you sustained income over the years. It may not be spectacular, but it should be steady.

Income Funds and Bond Funds

The objective of income funds is to provide shareholders with a constant stream of cash flow through investments in fixed-income securities, such as bonds and high-yielding common and preferred stocks. The portfolios of income and bond funds can include corporate bonds, guaranteed and nonguaranteed obligations of the federal government, and municipal bonds issued by states, cities, and local municipalities, among other higher-yielding investments. Yields in general fluctuate based on the level of economic activity in the country. For example, when there is a slow-growth economy with little inflationary pressure, then bonds and other fixed-income securities are in demand, and the prices of bonds increase and yields go down. The opposite is true when the economy is accelerating.

Convertible Bond Funds

An income fund that has an equity component to it is a *convertible bond fund*. It has been described as the best of two worlds primarily because convertible bonds with relatively high yields can convert into common stock under a specific set of circumstances. If the common stock's price goes up, the convertible bond price will follow, although not necessarily at the same percentage rate. Because convertible bond funds diversify, their portfolio can include many lower-grade bonds in an effort to entice new purchases of the fund's shares by offering a very high current return to investors. Be careful. If you like the idea of a convertible bond fund, you will sacrifice some yield for more stable, safer underlying securities in the fund's portfolio.

U.S. Government Securities Funds

A U.S. government securities fund gives the investor current income while the fund invests in federal agency securities and government notes and bonds having medium- to long-term maturities. The longer length of maturities will afford the fund a higher rate of return. But, by the same token, the fund's net asset value will be subjected to greater fluctuations as the interest rate structure in the country changes. Government bond funds, however, are very safe, and a small percentage of your total invested funds should be placed in this type of fund if its very conservative investment philosophy is consistent with yours.

Tax-Free Funds

Tax-free funds are usually made up of a portfolio which includes fixed-income securities issued by cities, states, counties, and other municipalities. Some tax-free funds are short-term (one to two years) maturity, others can be intermediate-term maturities extending from seven to ten years. Longer-term portfolios have maturities that extend to 20–30 years. Their objective is to produce current income that is tax-free to the owner of the shares. If you are in a high income tax bracket and prefer not to receive ordinary taxable income from sources such as corporate bonds, certificates of deposit, or government securities, you might welcome this type of mutual fund.

Index Funds

Index funds are mutual funds that emulate the stock and bond averages. The stock index fund tracks, for instance, the Standard and Poor's 500 stock index or the NASDAQ 100. A bond index fund attempts to match the broad-based bond market index. Although index funds aim to do as well as the comparable indexes they are attempting to match, they sometimes outperform and other times underperform that index because the manager holds in the fund's portfolio securities that are similarly *weighted*, but are not precisely the same as in the broad index.

All index funds are not exactly the same. Some funds follow an index devoted to large capitalization companies, others favor the smaller companies. Investors interested in technology stocks will be more inclined to purchase an index that emphasizes those issues. Other investors or trustees look for an index fund that seeks to replicate a growth stock index or seek a growth stock index, such as the Wilshire 5000, an index that consists of all U.S. publicly traded stock. The more successful index funds appear to be those that advertise the most and make the newspapers and the key investment periodicals, which add credibility to the fund but does not necessarily improve its performance. Indeed, check the historical background and record of the index fund's activities for the last five to seven years, and, if you believe in the concept of the index fund, see whether that particular fund mirrors your investment philosophy and objectives.

Index funds can indeed provide a conservative investor/trustee with excellent diversification that will duplicate the averages both in up and down markets. Their cost structure is also an attractive feature. In an active growth-oriented mutual fund, for instance, the turnover ratio can be 50–70 percent of the portfolio in one year. As a result, transaction costs are high for the fund and must be borne indirectly by the shareholders. In an index fund, however, the costs are appreciably lower and therefore the shareholders pay less in yearly management fees because an index fund doesn't require the micromanagement that a stock fund requires. The index fund sticks with the securities in the index and trades only when and if the index itself makes adjustments.

One of the more attractive features of an index fund is that a shareholder can invest in a very broad array of stocks or other types of securities without paying individual sales commissions. A drawback is that you generally have to stay with the losers that are in the index, but you also have the winners. It is a compromise and a balance that is attractive to many investors and trust administrators.

Why Mutual Funds Are a Good Choice

So far the various investment objectives that mutual funds offer have been discussed. What else, in addition to diversification and professional management, makes them a viable and attractive alternative to other forms of investments for the estate planner? They offer convenience and accommodation to both large and small investors by (1) maintaining records and submitting financial statements to share owners periodically, (2) accepting very small amounts and placing money into an investment that meets your objectives immediately, (3) adding capital gains and income distributions to your account automatically, and (4) providing a choice of investment objectives within a family of funds.

The net asset value of your mutual fund shares or those titled in a trust are easy to follow because bid and offered prices are quoted daily in most local newspapers. *Liquidity* is an added convenience allowing you to redeem shares at net asset value any day you wish with just a phone call. Because of the broad *diversification* of securities held in portfolios, mutual funds reduce risk below what is found in funds managed by investment counseling firms, trust companies, or banks whose selection process is somewhat more concentrated and directed toward fewer individual issues. Diversification also gives greater overall *safety.* As a matter of fact, if you would like more diversification, you can purchase shares in two or three funds with similar investment objectives, but characterized by a slightly different investment bent or style. This will increase your perspective but not change your investment objectives or level of risk.

Flexibility is another important advantage of mutual funds, which offer you a wide range of opportunities by allowing you to switch to another fund within a *family of funds* without incurring any substantial fees. As a prudent, cost-conscious investor and estate planner you need to

1. Check costs, including sales charges, management and redemption fees, especially if you choose to purchase no-load shares through a discount broker rather than directly through the fund. There may be additional costs such as distribution fees and deferred sales charges if and when you sell the shares. Be careful—read the prospectus. True no-load funds charge only a small management fee.
2. Determine if there is any pending litigation against the fund and what impact it might have.
3. Look at the latest annual report and prospectus for the portfolio of securities that the fund has invested in.
4. Identify the better performing and most suitable funds for you and your trust or retirement plan. Follow the performance of the funds for a period of time and get to know something about the managers. Who are they and what have they done in the field.

Mutual Fund Performance

In every mutual fund prospectus you will find information on the particular fund's performance for at least a ten year period. The results generally assume reinvestment of all capital gains and dividends for indicated periods. The returns shown do not allow for federal, state, or local taxes that shareholders must pay on a current basis. It would be wise to refer to the footnotes under the performance record to make doubly sure what the returns shown actually include or exclude.

If you wish to check comparative performance records of many mutual funds (and you should), there are various companies that monitor the industry, publish periodic reports, and provide rates of return and ranking. Several of the best known services are Weisenberger Investment Companies, Lipper Analytical, and Mutual Fund Forecaster. Others include *IBC/Donoghue's Mutual Funds Almanac* which provides a directory of funds, toll-free phone numbers, and a ten-year performance record of more than 4,000 funds. Another publication that offers important information is the *Morningstar Mutual Fund Sourcebook*, which does not predict the best investment for an individual to make, but does provide performance profiles, records, and historical information that are essential to making informed decisions. It also gives accurate measures of each fund's volatility and identifies investments that have been the best at providing investors with returns commensurate with the risks taken. All of these publications may be found in the financial section of your public library.

A Check-a-Month Plan

One of the primary reasons that you would invest in a mutual fund is for the purpose of increasing and maintaining a level of growth of principal, combined with consistent income earnings, that will give you a fund from which to receive periodic payments sent to you during your retirement years. To make these arrangements, a withdrawal application must be completed stating how much you would like to receive from your account. Payments can be in the usual form of a monthly check or it may be paid quarterly. The amount can increase or de-crease or can be stopped at any time depending on your needs. The monies would come from your original in-vestment in the mutual fund plus accumulated divi-dends, including capital gains and income earnings received over the years.

The big questions are judging the amount you and your spouse require to supplement your other income and the amount to withdraw from the mutual fund account. Much of it will have to do with the life expectancy of both of you, and the quality of life you wish to maintain. You will be better able to judge this later on and to make the proper adjustments to the amount to be taken in peri-odic checks.

Dollar-Cost Averaging

Dollar-cost averaging is often employed in the purchase of mutual fund shares. It is simply a practice of buying constant *dollar* amounts of a fund's shares at regular in-tervals regardless of price levels. This disciplined invest-ment technique bears out the conclusion that more shares of the fund are purchased at relatively low price levels than at high levels; consequently the average cost of all shares is lower. For this mathematically reliable concept to be successful, however, you should not stop buying shares when the securities markets fluctuate or are down and things look gloomy. This is exactly when to take advantage of dollar-cost averaging and acquire more shares at lower prices. Systematic share accumulation programs lend themselves ideally to dollar-cost averag-ing because periodic investment is not concerned with the market being up or down or historically high or low. Dollar-cost averaging has been successful over the years because the long-term trend of the stock market has risen.

Tax Reporting

Mutual funds are unique in the investment world because they do not pay taxes on realized capital gains, dividends, or interest received from their portfolio of securities. They don't pay these taxes because mutual funds are considered to be regulated investment companies and are required by law to distribute all of their investment earnings, thereby creating potential tax liabilities for their shareholders. The fund, in effect, acts as a conduit into which it takes capital gains and income from its investments and passes them on to you. As a shareholder whether or not you receive the distribution in cash or additional shares, you are obligated to pay federal, state, and local taxes, just as if you owned the various securities yourself. If you own shares in several different funds, each is treated as a single entity and for federal tax purposes reported separately. As an owner of shares, or if it is titled in the name of your trust, a 1099-Div fund statement will be sent to you indicating earnings received from the fund during the past year. Additionally, the amount you receive is also reported to the IRS in the year of the distribution.

Mutual funds will generally declare distributions of earnings to you and other shareholders on a particular date at the end of the year. If you are accumulating more shares, or even starting to acquire shares for a new account, knowing the date of the distribution can be significant. Your awareness should not deter you from buying shares under a plan of accumulation. But, if you are dollar-cost-averaging, or even attempting to buy on dips in the market, try to purchase the shares *after* the fund has declared its dividend, *not before* the distribution takes place. If you acquire the shares just before the date the fund declares a dividend you will be responsible for the payment of taxes for the entire amount of the distribution after perhaps only having owned the shares for a couple of days or weeks. If you wait until after the dividend declaration date, the share price will be lowered by the amount of the distribution and will have received more shares for the same amount of money and not paid taxes for that year.

Keeping all records of your mutual fund transactions is most important, for if you are not careful, it is possible to inadvertently pay taxes twice on the same distribution. For instance, paying taxes in the year the dividends are paid to you and then again at some later time when or if you sell the shares. If you do sell (redeem) shares at any time for yourself or as a trustee, you will have to identify the acquisition cost basis of the shares being sold and report gains or losses to the government at the end of the year. Although there are other methods to determine your basis, *the average cost, single category method* appears to be the easiest way to establish realized taxable gains and losses although it may not always produce the best tax result. The fund management will calculate average cost as a service and it will generally be shown on your periodic statements. If you need any further information regarding various cost-basis methods, consult your tax adviser or write to the IRS and ask for a copy of publication #564.

How to Open an Account

Shares of a *load fund* may be purchased through a conveniently located stock brokerage firm, which acts as an intermediary between you and the mutual fund management company for which the firm receives a percentage of the acquisition charge. *No-load funds*, on the other hand, sell their shares directly to the public. This means that there is no sales commission to you. The no-load fund does, however, have a management fee and administrative charges that can vary between .5 and 1.50 percent. This amount is appreciably less than the 8.5–9.5 percent acquisition and management fee charged by load funds on small purchases. You should check and compare those fees very carefully.

True, it is somewhat more difficult to purchase shares of a no-load fund because they are not sold through easily accessible retail stock brokerage firms. You can, however, obtain information on no-load funds in your public library, through advertisements in newspapers, or by writing to the No-Load Mutual Fund Association at Valley Forge, PA 19481. The association is a nonprofit organization comprised of investment companies, and it would furnish you with a list of no-load mutual funds, including addresses and phone numbers.

A publication that lists both load and no-load funds is entitled *The Investor's Guide to Low Cost Mutual Funds*, and it can be obtained through writing 1900 Erie Street, Suite 120, Kansas City, MO 64116-3465. *The Membership Directory of the 100% No-load Mutual Fund Council* can be obtained by writing to Mutual Fund Council, 1501 Broadway, Suite 1809, New York, NY 10036. After receiving these directories you may then write or call a specific fund or funds requesting sales literature, the latest annual report, a prospectus, and an application form to open an account. Make a point to read the prospectus carefully. It contains such important facts as the fund's investment objectives and policy, the original offering price of the shares, and such pertinent financial information as the date of issuance, financial structure of the company issuing shares, and allocation of assets in its portfolio. In the sales literature, you will also be given the opportunity to select whether to receive your dividends in cash or to reinvest them. Capital gains distributions may also be reinvested.

If you are investing for a trust, as trustee, and have decided to open an account and commit monies to a particular fund or funds, you are usually required to send the first and last pages of the trust document. Do not send in the original. A copy to the management company for signature and name verification should suffice.

Selecting a Plan

A voluntary accumulation plan, a contractual plan, or a check-a-month plan are various plans you may select. Generally, the initial minimum investment is $1,000–$2,500, but it could be less depending on the fund. Thereafter, your payments are mailed to the custodian bank with minimum individual investments of about $100–$250, which will purchase as many shares as possible at the daily quoted offering price. Investors have a great deal of flexibility as to reinvesting or receiving dividends and capital gains distributions. Load and no-load mutual funds will send share ownership certificates to you, but in most cases they are not issued or mailed to the owner unless requested.

The Custodian Bank and Its Functions

Most mutual funds retain qualified financial institutions, such as a national bank or trust company, to act as custodian. The custodian bank performs several functions:

1. It pays out dividends to shareholders.
2. It acts as transfer agent.
3. It acts as registrar for the fund.
4. It holds cash and securities of the fund.
5. It performs certain clerical services.

6. It receives payments from investors and invests those payments in mutual fund shares.
7. It can act as custodian for the investors' shares if shareholders do not wish to hold the shares.
8. It keeps books and records.

The custodian bank does not perform any sales functions of fund shares, nor does it distribute shares. It also does not perform any investment or money management services specifically related to the mutual fund.

Closed-End Funds

The mutual funds that were just discussed were open-end funds that buy and sell securities on behalf of their shareholders. The choice of securities in the portfolio depends on the money manager's outlook on the stocks, bonds, or money market instruments and reflects the current economic trend and the manager's evaluation of that trend. The value of the shares that you or a trust own fluctuates from one day to the next and increases or decreases with the share prices of underlying securities in the portfolio.

A *closed-end fund*, also known as a closed-end investment company, is similar to the open-end fund in that it can provide you or your trust with an opportunity to invest indirectly in a diversified portfolio of securities. Whereas the open-end fund can issue as many shares as it chooses, the closed-end fund has a fixed amount of capital and an authorized amount of issued common stock that is also fixed. These shares are not sold directly by the company to the public or institutions, but must be purchased just like other individual shares of stock, generally through a retail stock brokerage firm. Additionally, the closed-end fund does not stand ready to redeem its shares as mutual funds do. The price of the shares of closed-end funds varies and reflects the daily quoted price of the underlying shares behind the closed-end fund's common stock. In addition to the fund selling its shares to the public, it can also raise capital by floating debt securities in the form of bonds, in a manner similar to that of any other corporation. A closed-end fund, therefore, builds leverage into its capital structure by using borrowed funds for investment purposes. This, of course, cannot be done by an open-end mutual fund.

Funds of this type generally sell at a discount from net asset value, so if the market value of all the underlying securities is divided by the number of outstanding shares, the price of its shares will be at a price below its net asset value. Two reasons closed-end funds sell at a discount from net are that the shares are not sold as aggressively as open-end mutual funds are and the performance history of closed-end funds is somewhat suspect because many of them collapsed (as did many other types of securities) in the aftermath of 1929. Having large blocks of securities in their portfolios for sale during that time made selling not only difficult but impossible, except at much lower prices. Consequently, some historically minded investors are still somewhat shy of them.

A closed-end fund, however, can provide a good total rate of return, sometimes as much or more than the income-oriented mutual funds. You are able to receive a return of $100 in assets that the fund owns, even though you may be paying as little as $90–95 in some cases for those assets because of the discount. Also, a closed-end fund can be purchased with ordinary stock exchange commissions, which may be negotiated at a reduced or discounted rate. There is no 8 percent or 9.25 percent basic acquisition fee, as is required in the purchase of most load open-end mutual funds.

Although closed-end funds were less than inspiring performers in the 1970s and 1980s, their discounts from net asset value seem to have contracted somewhat in the 1990s, which would indicate that they are receiving greater investment interest and acceptability by the investing public and professionals currently.

A final word on open-end mutual funds: In general they are excellent vehicles for you or your trust to receive skilled professional management at low cost. They provide diversification to reduce risk, asset allocation strategies, and record keeping; they furnish monthly activity reports and year-end tax statements, reinvest capital gains and income if you wish, and generally provide you or your trustee with an easy way to invest. If you like the idea, select the mutual fund(s) whose management style and strategy best fits your own. After all, you are the one who dictates the investment parameters that later on will be entrusted to your successor. This investment posture is set forth by you in the trust document and must be followed until all assets are distributed to beneficiaries after your death.

Convenience of Estate Settlement

Another good reason to consider owning a mutual fund as an investment is *the convenience of estate settlement.* Having a variety of stocks or bonds in your portfolio makes it a little more difficult and time consuming for an executor or a successor trustee to liquidate. In addition, some shares of perhaps smaller companies may not be easily marketable when they must be sold. Mutual fund shares, are very easily liquidated. A further advantage of mutual fund ownership is how much more simple it is to divide open-end mutual fund shares than individually held shares of stock among the various beneficiaries.

This allows little or no disruption in the quality of diversification that is such an important safety feature in investing.

Maintaining Your Income Stream

There is perhaps no more important objective during the postmortem period than for your successor trustee to maintain the income stream for spouse and beneficiaries. Your successor, as described in the "powers of the trustee" section of the trust document, shall continue to act as manager or provide oversight functions of the trust. In this regard, it is incumbent upon the successor (whether it be an individual or a firm managing a portfolio of securities, a mutual fund, a bank or trust company, or an executor) to see that sufficient revenue, based on a consistent total rate of return from trust investments, be present and continuing. Any loss or decline in trust principal because of poor investment strategies can ultimately reduce the asset base and therefore jeopardize trust income that may be needed later on. Asset management should therefore be taken seriously because it is critical to the success or failure of the program. If it fails, it can cause financial harm to the very person(s) you wish to protect.

9

Trust Administration and Supervision

In the preceding chapter both open-end mutual funds and closed-end funds were discussed in terms of personal and professional investment management as it applies to risk and return, asset guidelines and strategy, selectivity, safety and asset allocation methods, among other things. It was established that a mutual fund investment is a good choice for an estate planner because it provides low cost professional management and basically transfers the responsibility of making investment decisions from you to the fund managers and financial analysts. Some other ways that you can provide yourself and your family with investment expertise and administration and asset supervision will be discussed in this chapter, although from the slightly different perspective of using such financial institutions as commercial banks, trust companies, and large stock brokerage firms to provide for your estate needs.

What Services Do Financial Institutions Provide?

Most service-oriented financial institutions are specifically set up to furnish the investor and estate planner with a wide range of services. Banks, for instance, in addition to basic checking, savings, and money market accounts, provide mortgages and home improvement loans, automobile loans, and other consumer credit, personal, business, and farm loans. They have services involving clearing and transferring of funds, issue letters of credit for international trade, and offer trust, investment, and custodian services, among other miscellaneous banking services. These banks have taken the name full service banks.

In addition, they provide to their clients special accounts such as tax-sheltered retirement programs, Keogh plans for the self-employed, individual retirement accounts (IRAs). Group IRAs, corporate and partnership accounts, and accounts under the Gift to Minors Act, to name a few. A Gift to Minors account, for example, can be opened in your name as custodian for your child or grandchild. The account would read, "John Doe as custodian for Mary Doe under the Uniform Gift to Minors Act (UGMA) of (the state in which you live)."

Commercial banks can also have trust powers. Trust powers, however, can only be exercised if certain state requirements for fiduciaries are met by the bank in addition to basic monetary requirements, such as adequate capital and surplus. Generally, the institution is required to establish a separate trust department not directly connected with its commercial banking activities and is subject to scrutiny by examiners of the Comptroller of the Currency or the Board of Governors of the Federal Reserve. The commercial bank also provides money management and estate planning services for its trust clients.

Trust Companies

Trust companies, on the other hand, are separate institutions and have no affiliation with commercial banks per se. They do not offer banking services as such, but concentrate on asset management, financial planning and analysis, tax planning, and managing of real estate. They may act as an executor of an estate, and as a trustee and do estate planning, analyze insurance policies for possible improvement of coverage, do net worth analysis, and may act as an authorized agent to represent a principal in the conduct or liquidation of a business. The trust company may be an administrator appointed by the probate court, act as a custodian for the physical care and handling of securities, receive dividends or interest, and disburse the cash to the proper individuals. It may even pay bills and arrange allowances for families. In a strictly technical sense, trust companies handle those activities that are necessary in the relationship that exists between the trustor/grantor, and the trustee (the trust company). The trustor commits the property to the trustee, who administers it for the benefit of the named beneficiary.

Because of their increased incomes and the concomitant accumulation of wealth, many people have turned to trust companies for services. This has contributed to their enormous growth in the last decade. Even those people who have estates of moderate size are becoming more aware of how trust companies and bank trust departments can help them not only currently, but also plan the disposition of their estate at some later date.

Large stock brokerage houses also have started to provide trust services to their clients but the services to date have not been as all-inclusive as banks and trust companies. The scope of their services and main efforts are still concentrated in the development of retail sales of securities and other financial instruments by branches spread throughout the country.

As one who is interested in trust asset management, administrative support services, accounting, and estate planning, it might be prudent for you to know who is

going to handle your account. At the financial institution
you choose, who *are* the money managers and what has
been their record of achievement over the last ten years?
What is their basic investment philosophy and are they
willing to spend a certain amount of time with your trust
officer to develop an appropriate investment strategy for
you and help institute an estate plan that is well con-
ceived?

Trust officers always seem to have suggestions as to
what you can do to develop and promote an estate plan.
In most cases, they will do this without charging you a
fee because they want your trust business. Listen to what
the trust representative has to say and compare it with
your own research and knowledge. Does it make sense to
you? If the representative suggests that an insurance trust
or a living trust should be established, spend some time
with the idea and do some reading and rereading on the
subject until you feel confident that you understand why
you are doing it. What are the advantages and disadvantages of this approach? After you have made the proper
preliminary choice you might check it over with your attorney for validation or rejection before you do anything
that is legally binding.

If you believe that a financial institution can help you,
it would be wise to look at several different banks or trust
companies and make a comparison to determine which
one has the most comprehensive and cost-effective service for your particular needs. It is a good idea to do this
research while you are still active and not beset by any
health problems. It might also be wise to have your
spouse participate in your decision-making process. Indeed, there may come a time in your life when the sole
responsibility of managing your portfolio, record keeping, and doing taxes becomes a chore and you or your
spouse no longer have the inclination or desire to do
these things. The question then becomes who will take

on that responsibility? Will it be a brother, a sister, your son or daughter, a good friend or perhaps a bank, trust company, or brokerage firm that can take over the financial management and administration of your investments. If, for example, it is a trust company or bank, it would be a good idea to talk to the people that you and your spouse will be dealing with and try to find out the temperament and personality traits that the trust officer or your individual administrator appears to have. Do you get the feeling that the person handling your account will be easy to talk with and take a personal interest in your family's financial situation. If not, then go someplace else. It is critical that you and your spouse have a high degree of rapport with those who will be making important decisions regarding your family welfare.

The Custodial Arrangement

What types of accounts are available at banks and trust companies? Suppose you are not willing to give up total control over the investment and administration of your assets even though they are now under a living trust? There is a custodial type arrangement that you might consider agreeing to with a corporate trustee. It allows *you* to manage your assets, but it provides some relief from the administrative record keeping associated with personal investing and management. The financial institution will act as your agent in the protection, care, and custody of your assets. It will execute buy and sell orders for securities, furnish transaction confirmations, collect dividends and investment income, make available safe-keeping of securities, disburse payments to individuals as instructed, provide periodic activity statements and send you tax information at the end of the year for income tax preparation. In addition, a large bank or trust company, because of the volume of business, can also claim to provide securities transactional costs at reduced rates somewhat similar to what large institutional investors pay.

In a nutshell, this type of account allows you to make the investment decisions and the financial institution handles the details. But is this much more than you would receive from a full-service stock brokerage firm? Perhaps not entirely, but the emphasis is different. *Custodial services at a trust company will focus on your entire estate rather than concentrate on merely securities transactions.* The account executive at a stock brokerage firm usually knows little to nothing about trusts or tax and estate planning. The trust officer, on the contrary, does it every day. So when you reach the point in your life when you choose not to make investment decisions, nor do any management or bookkeeping, the financial institution will take over and do it for you. You will have to sign an agreement with the institution as to the level of services you would like. The trust department will then take over the management of your investment portfolio based on an agreed level of risk consistent with your investment objectives. This can be done on an informal basis that generally requires only a simple letter of instructions designating the financial institution to act as your investment agent. The letter would require goals to be established that would then allow the financial manager to select specific shares of stock of various companies to be purchased and placed in your account.

Dealing with a trust company steeped in tradition and having a long history of trust management may give you the safety and security that you need. In addition, banking or trust officers have a closer connection with the financial analysts doing the actual investing. They can be "right down the hall." And if there are any questions on investment strategy and selection the answers would be readily available to you.

Full-Trust Services

Banks and trust companies, and now also trust departments of large stock brokerage firms, not only perform custodial and money management services, but also full-trust services that can even involve funeral arrangements and locating and filing your last will and testament. Below is a list of complete services that they will perform if you are an executor of an estate, for administrators representing you as your family's interests, or as a trustee, cotrustee, or successor trustee, and as a custodian. Costs for the services listed below are not shown because they vary from institution to institution in different parts of the country and can be adjusted at any time by individual institutions. Services are also more expensive when they are considered to be more complex and time consuming than the ordinary. You need to go over the trust agreement very carefully before committing yourself legally. As you can see below, the services involve a whole array of individual options that you can choose from, or you can just buy an entire package. The financial institution will act as custodian of assets of the estate, including assets held in safekeeping, and provide for

1. income being collected and recorded;
2. periodic statements of transactions;
3. periodic deposits in checking account;
4. itemized statements of taxable income, including capital gains and losses;
5. temporary investment of cash;
6. availability of negotiated brokerage commissions on sales of securities;

7. execution and/or settlement of all security trades;
8. registration, reregistration and security transfers;
9. additional transaction statements and investment performance statements;
10. collection of all income, dividends, and interest with credit to client accounts;
11. automatic cash management and investment in short-term instruments based on client instructions;
12. furnishing statements, market values, and projected annual income;
13. distribution of assets, including obtaining receipts for service;
14. payment of bills and disbursement of funds as directed;
15. wire transfers and cash sweeps to or from other accounts;
16. applying for and collecting insurance proceeds and other death benefits plus social security and veteran's benefits;
17. payment of money market interest on all idle and transient cash balances;
18. preparation of decedent's final income tax return, federal and state income tax returns;
19. preparation of fiduciary income tax return, federal and state income tax returns;
20. preparation of federal estate tax return;
21. preparation of state inheritance tax return;
22. preparation of court reports, inventory accounting, and each additional accounting;
23. postmortem tax planning;
24. evaluation of creditors' claims and defense of unjust claims;
25. payment of legacies; and
26. special planning for closely held business inter-

ests and real estate, including arranging for sale when necessary.

Collective Investment Funds

If you choose *not* to have individual shares of stock of various companies purchased for your separate portfolio, you have an option to participate with other investment accounts at the financial institution. These accounts are called the *collective investment funds* and provide clients with a variety of investment options having different objectives and levels of risk to choose from. The collective funds, in some cases, are not managed by an in-house staff of financial analysts but by outside money management teams or investment advisers that provide this service to financial institutions. Your trust account's investment in the collective fund(s) of your choice is subject to regular investment fees and expenses. The charges may vary slightly among institutions, and it is important for you to compare the services offered. It may be that one institution will charge a little more but offer more to you. But having the appropriate investment mix consistent with your risk tolerance and establishing a good working relationship with your trust officer or individual administrator are very important for the proper functioning of your account.

The collective or comingled investment funds under management by the financial institution are distinguished from one another by their different investment objectives and levels of risk in ways very similar to the earlier mutual fund descriptions. Your investment in the fund of your choice allows you to participate in the success or failure of the fund's program. If you are not sure of your specific objectives, the manager will try to blend several of the collective funds to satisfy your risk tolerance and investment point of view. Some institutions will permit this blending as a service for both small and large portfolios.

Although there would appear to be little risk in having your funds at a financial institution, recent history has told us that we should be very careful wherever we place our assets. Cash and securities kept in safekeeping at trust companies and banks and administered by the institution are placed in segregated accounts, distinguished from the institution's own assets under strict audit control, and cannot be reached by creditors of the bank or trust company. FDIC insurance, however, for a trust account, is generally limited to uninvested cash and insured up to $100,000 for each beneficiary or owner represented. Financial institutions that deal in trust services are held to very high regulatory standards and compliance oversight by not only bank auditors, but also by outside accounting firms and by the comptroller of the currency. In addition, the majority of financial institutions carry errors and omission indemnity insurance to protect themselves against claims by others.

Granted that investment risk cannot be totally eliminated, a conservatively managed account can be one of the primary advantages in dealing with a large and stable financial institution because it has a strong balance sheet, solid management, and years of business experience. If one particular individual that you have been dealing with leaves the firm, another perhaps even more suitable can take that administrator's place with no loss of continuity or service. Most large institutions want your business and will generally make whatever slight adjustments you need to make you a satisfied client. When the business of estate settlement begins, having an experienced and knowledgeable bank administrator or trust officer to deal with, especially one that knows your account, will be a great help to your executor or personal representative. Your beneficiaries also will be helped when relating to the management of assets and distributions of property at some future period.

Indeed, having a corporate trustee professionally manage your assets and provide many of the services that were discussed here can be very helpful to you and your spouse and family later on. Some people, however, who have done their own investing for years find it difficult to give up any type of control over their money. Many have been very successful on their own without any outside advice. But the temperament required and the time involved with record keeping and decision making can make it a burden, especially when you want to spend your time doing other things.

A financial institution can generally oversee these financial functions. It is what they do all the time. True, they can make mistakes in investing and trading securities, but they can be more objective about their decisions. They don't have the emotional tie that the ordinary investor has to his or her portfolio. The professional manager can sell a stock at a loss without a blink of an eye. The relationship, however, between the investor and his or her hard earned money becomes very serious business and manifests an intimate, almost mystical quality about protecting assets, but more importantly not diminishing capital.

In earlier chapters, ways and means to reduce death taxes by the use of strategic estate-planning devices were examined. Just as important, however, is the maintenance of the growth of the principal value of the assets invested in your trust that will provide income to the surviving spouse sometime in the future. Trust companies and banks have been providing this service for years. Admittedly, some institutions have been more successful than others. Find one that has had a consistent record of positive total returns over the years and that fits in with your other estate-planning objectives. It might be a good time to consider trust management and administration seriously and make it an integral part of your overall estate plan.

10

Ownership of Property and Titling of Assets

As noted in an earlier chapter, one can effectively eliminate or substantially reduce estate administration and property transfer costs by not having any assets titled in one's name. Another way is to place the property beyond the jurisdiction of the court. This doesn't mean that you need to place whatever you own into someone else's name to escape eventual tax liability. Clearly, though, it does suggest that some strategic estate planning as to titling and ownership of assets that you hold may be wise.

How Is Your Property Titled?

Before you can establish any sensible estate plan, you must know how your property is presently owned. That is, who or what entity has legal title to your car, vacation home, your domicile (legal residence), certain stocks, bonds, insurance, bank accounts, certificates of deposit, mutual funds, etc. Have you looked lately? Property can be owned outright in your name as sole owner or it may be held in your name with another name or names showing that the other person or persons have a financial interest in the property. Assets held in this manner

147

generally pass to the surviving owner outside your probatable estate. For example, many people use joint tenancy arrangements at banks for the purpose of convenience, especially when they get older and can't get around the way they had in the past. The other person on the account can help pay bills, cash checks, and do other administrative tasks that may be required. Also, this kind of joint bank account has been employed in the past as an easy means of passing assets to heirs and others. There can, however, be significant drawbacks to having bank accounts or other forms of property such as real estate in joint names.

As a case in point, would anyone in your family be surprised or even shocked if it were found out that in her will your mother left the family home to you and your brothers but it was discovered later that the property had, in fact, been titled not in her name alone but jointly with her second husband (not your father) as owners? This has happened in the past. Who received the property? Did it pass under the terms of the will? No! Ownership went directly to the joint owner, your mother's husband. It should be made clear, then, that every type of asset you have an ownership interest in, must be scrutinized as to how you wish it to be titled, and what property will or will not pass under the terms of your will. Joint tenancy and tenancy in common should be designated to make title clear. For example, let the title read Mr. Henry H. Jones and Mr. John P. Smith as *tenants* in common. If you own the asset yourself, it should read Mrs. Henry H. Jones as sole owner.

Joint Ownership of Property

Joint ownership may be the most popular way of transferring property at death and, in addition, avoid the probate process. Although the actual passing of property takes place legally at the death of the joint tenant, it is basically the result of a transfer that took place during one's lifetime but only if it was, in fact, a valid joint tenancy. The property then becomes the survivor's, and any property interest that the decedent might have had disappears.

Under one type of joint ownership such as a joint tenancy with rights of survivorship (JTWRS), each tenant owns 100 percent of the assets and at death of the first survivor the property goes directly to the surviving tenant by operation of law. If there happens to be an existing will in which the decedent attempts to give to someone else his or her interest in this particular asset, the attempt of the will shall fail and surviving tenant becomes the owner immediately at the death of the first tenant. As an example, if you have a joint checking account with the rights of survivorship, there is no interruption in the use of the account when one of the tenants dies. What happens if both or all the tenants die simultaneously in an auto accident? The effect is that the joint tenancy becomes a tenancy in common and each deceased tenant would have that portion of his or her estate subject to probate. The disposition of property according to the wills of each of the tenants must be taken into account.

The use of a joint tenancy arrangement is an inexpensive and easy way for both married and unmarried persons to own titled property. It can, however, be full of legal hazards simply because you don't know what your co-owner will do regarding his or her ownership rights. Joint tenancy may be employed more prudently for spouses who are more likely than others to agree on the disposition of certain co-owned assets at some later date. But it may be foolhardy to do a joint tenancy arrangement with a son or daughter for convenience sake with either one or both having different ideas as to what to do with the property and when certain monies are to be used. For this reason great care must be taken in using this type of account when there is the possibility of a gift that may lead to a taxable event.

For example, you decide it would be appropriate to make a gift to your son. By gifting him an asset, you will reduce the value of your taxable estate, escape probate on the amount of the gift, and provide your son with some financial help sometime in the future when he needs it to raise a family. But the transfer must in fact take place. As an example, some money in your account is held by a stock broker and titled in "street" name. You and your son sign the account card for opening a joint account and you give instructions to the stockbroker to purchase 1,000 shares of General Motors (GM) stock from the money transferred into the new account. Who now owns the shares? Did you make a completed gift to your son of 500 shares of GM stock plus half of whatever else, such as residual cash, that went into the account? Let's see what happened. Four months went by and your son contacted the broker and asked for his portion of the GM dividend payments. He also placed an order to sell 300 of "his" shares when the price reached a certain level. Did your son take control and assume ownership of the 500 shares? It would appear that he did. In this case, there is a high probability that you would be subject to gift tax liability on the amount gifted in excess of the $10,000 annual exclusion. By withdrawing the funds from the sale with no apparent obligation to notify you, the donor, your son showed that he took control of the gift. It is not exactly what you had in mind, but the gift was complete. Doing this through a brokerage house where the securities are held in the street (broker's) name has been questioned as a proper method to make gifts by the IRS.

If the situation were changed somewhat and the father established a similar account in which the son did nothing but sign the account card and after that never contacted the broker, made no attempt to use any of the earnings in the account, and never reported any income from the account, one would have to argue that this account was set up by the father for his convenience in which he never really gave up control of the shares and that in fact there was no completed gift clearly established. Therefore, no gift tax needs to be paid. The IRS contends that this type of arrangement would be like a joint bank account arrangement established by one person in which the ownership of funds remains in the hands of the person opening, maintaining, and controlling the account.

Joint ownership can indeed have its drawbacks. As a further example, Mr. and Mrs. Jones bought some shares of stock that the broker placed into an account showing both names and titled as joint tenants with rights of survivorship. This was intended to keep the shares out of the probate process. Perfectly legitimate and perfectly proper reasoning. After Mr. Jones died, there was no problem in registering the shares in the name of Mrs. Jones as sole surviving owner. At a later date, when Mrs. Jones sold some of the shares she found that she was taxed what she considered to be "too much." The IRS told her it had something to do with joint ownership. What had happened was that when Mr. and Mrs. Jones bought the shares several years before they paid $10 per share for 200 shares of General Foods Corporation the stock was registered in both names. At Mr. Jones's death the valuation was $50 per share but "stepping up" the cost basis to fair market value is permitted under current law and should have eliminated any capital gains tax. The shares, however, were in joint tenancy and because they were in both names, *when one dies only half of the tax base steps up to market value.* Here, the tax combined basis was $2,000. The shares at the death of Mrs. Jones were 200 shares × $50 per share for a total value

of $10,000. The cost basis on half the shares steps up to
$5,000 ($50×100). When added to the husband's original investment, it makes the total cost basis $6,000. A
tax, therefore, must be paid on the remaining $4,000. So,
for a joint tenancy with right of survivorship between
husband and wife the rule under current law is that the
surviving spouse's basis, in this case Mrs. Jones's, includes one half of her husband's interest in the shares
fixed at fair market value for estate tax purposes.

Where property is held under a joint tenancy by husband and wife with rights of survivorship (JTWRS), the
property is treated for estate tax purposes as being owned
50 percent by each spouse, no matter which of the
spouses originally paid for it. This is known as the special 50 percent rule. If property is held under JTWRS
with a person other than your spouse, then the entire
amount is generally taxed as part of your estate unless
there is proof that the person actually contributed to the
joint account. Verification must be established as to how
much was contributed and when it took place. Keep in
mind then that anytime you own, transfer, or title property, you must always consider the potential gift and estate taxes involved.

Another form of joint tenancy—*tenants by the entirety*—is basically the same as JTWRS except that it can
only be used by husband and wife. Here also, the surviving spouse automatically becomes the sole owner of the
property at the death of the other. The property is equally
owned by both, and neither spouse can alter the ownership or give away, sell it, or place it into a trust without
the other's consent.

Tenancy in common allows each tenant to own the percentage of the property that each has paid for unless it is
stated otherwise in the ownership agreement. If it is not
stated and there are two tenants, then each tenant is assumed to own half. On the death of one of the owners,

the deceased owner's share goes through his or her probated estate and passes to beneficiaries as is provided in the will.

Even though joint ownership has been mentioned in several different forms, it should not be concluded that it is a substitute for a living trust or a will. You should consider the following points if you intend to employ joint ownership.

1. You cannot give away your interest in a joint tenancy in a will. Assets owned in joint tenancy belong to the owner that survives.

2. If you are a joint owner with someone, and you die without having sufficient funds to pay personal debts or taxes that are in your name, then *joint* assets can be used to satisfy those debts. In other words, the property is subject to claims of creditors. If the creditor lawsuits are successful, then the sale of assets may be required.

3. If you put someone else's name, such as a friend or neighbor, on a joint bank account or stock certificate because you may need their comfort or help, at your death you may unintentionally disinherit your children or others because the jointly owned assets go to the survivor.

4. A joint account doesn't provide for management of assets after you die. Nor can you have a planned program of distribution of income or principal.

5. There are no provisions to prevent outright and immediate receipt of property by the surviving owner.

6. The original owner or depositor can be subject to gift tax liability if the amount of the gift exceeds the $10,000 per year limitation and he or she appears to be the only contributor.

7. Joint tenancy arrangements usually lack investment flexibility that a trust offers.

8. The property cannot be transferred unless each co-tenant agrees.

9. And most important, if you are married and employ a joint tenancy arrangement, you can inadvertently lose one of the $600,000 lifetime exemption equivalents.

Partnerships

Having a partnership interest in either real or personal property is another type of ownership that should be introduced as part of your overall planning. Because there can be tax and legal consequences associated with all different types of ownership, you should review how your property is titled and whether or not a change from one type to another may be appropriate.

A partnership arrangement can be established by any two adults that have a business goal. The general partner is responsible for the everyday operations of the partnership entity and is legally responsible for claims against the partnership. The limited partners have limited rights, limited liability, and are not liable for any debts or losses incurred by the partnership. They can only lose the investment that they made. A partnership itself is not subject to the payment of income taxes because tax liability is passed through to the individual partners on any income earnings or losses the partnership incurs. The agreement that you sign with your other partners should state what will happen if and when your partner dies. Will the survivors continue the business? Will the ownership interest go to children? What formula to value your share was established initially in the shareholder agreement? Will your share after your death be placed in trust for the benefit of your beneficiaries? There are many possibilities that can take place. Your interest in the partnership after your death will have to be accounted for by the remaining partners and the extent of that interest will have to be substantiated. Partnership shares can be held in joint names or in the name of a trust in order to avoid probate.

Establishing a partnership can be one way to promote some of your estate-planning goals. For instance, if you establish yourself as a general partner and you own a large tract of land or an office building, you can shift various percentages of your interest each year to other family members (if you don't have the money to give or choose not to use cash to make gifts). The interest, however, given every year, must be below the $10,000 annual exclusion limit to insure that there will be no tax liability to you.

Another way to effectively benefit family members is to have the partnership entity purchase a life insurance policy on the life of a partner or partners. If and when a partner dies and if the proceeds are payable to or for the benefit of the partnership, then the proceeds of the insurance are not includable in the partner's gross estate. This, however, only applies if the partner (decedent) in his or her individual capacity has not had any incidents of ownership in the policy. If this is shown to be true, all the insurance proceeds must then be part of the decedent partner's estate and the appropriate tax paid on the proceeds. More about this in the chapter on insurance.

Community Property

Most of the discussions on property so far have been related to states in which common law ownership applies, that is, where the spouse whose name is on the checking account, the home, or a stock certificate, has legal title to the asset. When one spouse dies, the state generally will require a certain percentage of the decedent spouse's property to go to the surviving spouse. This is called the "spouse's minimum share." There are states, however, that have community property laws in which each spouse automatically owns one-half of the couple's property. It is not important in whose name the property is titled or whether it is a home, a certificate of deposit (CD) at a bank, or a paycheck; when married, each spouse owns half. The exception to the rule would involve property such as gifts or inheritances given to one spouse before marriage, or other property acquired prior to the date of the marriage. And how do the probate laws affect community property? Even if you will all of your property to your spouse after you die, your half of the estate ordinarily must be probated. You may, however, create a trust and place one-half the property under the trust's name. In addition, your spouse may also contribute one half to the trust. This method would escape probate costs.

One of the advantages of holding community property is that it receives a 100 percent step-up in tax basis for each half upon the death of either spouse as compared to a joint tenancy arrangement in which the step-up is on only the decedent's share of ownership. The property title, however, must show "C/P," community property. One negative that you should be aware of is that under community property either spouse can give away his or her share without the other spouse's knowledge or permission.

If you live in a community property state a further study of advantages and disadvantages would be worthwhile. There are currently eight community property states: Arizona, California, Idaho, Louisiana, Nevada, New Mexico, Texas, and Washington. Wisconsin also uses the "C/P" concept but is not technically a community property state.

Totten Trusts (Transfer on Death Accounts)

Another type of property ownership is similar to the JTWRS and is legally known as a Totten trust. It also has been called a payable-on-death (POD) account, and more currently a transfer-on-death (TOD) account. This type of revocable living trust without the formality of trust agreement is usually employed by the small depositor at a bank with no difficulty and at no expense. It is a form of ownership that allows the account at death to pass to the surviving owner by operation of law.

A TOD account is generally established when one person who has sole right and control, deposits funds into a bank account while both holders are still alive. At the death of the one that opened the account, the monies may or may not pass to the survivor. It would depend to a great extent on what the deposit agreement stated when the account was originally opened and an interpretation of local law. Did the person opening the account and depositing the money actually intend to have the other person own half of the funds? Or was the account opened so the other person would act as an agent, make deposits and withdrawals, pay bills, etc., for the original depositor? The intent here is the key.

When accounts of this type have been litigated, courts have ruled that the person added to the account was placed there to assure a level of convenience and the original depositor never intended that ownership (part or whole) should pass to the survivor. As a result, courts have concluded that the property must be distributed not by operation of law but under the terms of the will. It is an area in which the intentions of the parties is important. However, because the accounts generally do not involve large amounts of money and are used by small depositors, the IRS doesn't pursue them with great enthusiasm.

To make the requirements for TOD accounts clearer, some states now require that notification be given to owner-beneficiaries if their name is placed on the account. Other states require that the spouse of the original depositor has the right to share in the account assets regardless of who the other owner-beneficiary is. In general, in order to collect the funds in the account, the survivor needs to show a certified copy of the death certificate and proper identification. Money in a Totten trust deposited in a bank is covered by FDIC insurance up to $100,000 if the survivor is either a child, a grandchild, or the spouse of the original depositor.

Current information as to the implications of establishing this type of account is required by the depositor. TODs have enjoyed some popularity over the years by those who were familiar with them, and new legislation may be enacted to establish clearer rules and regulations and to broaden out ownership guidelines. States are approving legislation involving ownership of all types of securities under TOD agreements. So, in the future you will be permitted to register your stock, bonds, and mutual funds under an account that will read Sam Smith, TOD, Jane Smith, subject to Securities Transfer Association (STA) rules.

Registration of Securities and Other Financial Instruments

So far in this chapter some of the different forms of property ownership have been touched upon including single form, joint tenancy, under a trust, a partnership arrangement, community property, and the TOD account. Also discussed were the ramifications of registering and titling property by gift or by simply creating an entity in which you hold assets with other people. Any arrangement has pitfalls, and you should be aware of how and under what circumstances you should initiate the titling of assets you own. The point is to reduce the number of errors that take place in the transfer and registration of assets so that you and your spouse and family are not left unnecessarily vulnerable to tax liability and emotional discomfort.

After you have decided on how to best hold property— cash, securities, mutual fund shares, your home, etc., you must have these assets registered properly. We cannot discuss every possibility, but several might help. As an example, let's say you wish to purchase some mutual fund shares. You must complete an enrollment form that describes how you would title the shares. In the most simplistic terms, registration defines ownership: who will control and who will make investment decisions regarding the timing and number of shares purchased as well as other management decisions. If the account is listed in your name alone and your social security number is on the account, then it is referred to as a *single account*, and shares cannot be redeemed by anyone except you. In the event of your death, a personal representative would carry out your instructions, as stated in your will, with the shares going to a named beneficiary or beneficiaries.

You may also register the shares with other persons as joint tenants. A *joint tenancy account*, generally opened with a spouse or family member, can also be opened with number of joint owners. More than two or three persons would make the operation of the account cumbersome as any one of the owners listed on the registration could call for information on the account, and all the owners listed on the account would have to endorse redemption checks if some of the shares were sold because the rights of survivorship clause makes the assets in the account pass to the surviving owner(s) when any one of the other titled owners dies.

A trust account is also a possibility for your planning. Such an account is set up in the trust's name, and mutual fund or other assets are given to the trustee to manage for your benefit. You, however, may be your own trustee, or the account may be given to a corporate trustee. In any event, a copy of the trust document duly prepared and executed detailing its provisions must be given to the mutual fund. Some funds only require the first and last pages of the document, but at death a complete copy is required. Also, a trust account allows you to be very specific in naming beneficiaries. Any registration of property can be changed provided you have signed and executed the proper papers. To change title for a mutual fund account, you will need to send a letter of instruction defining the change in registration and sign a new enrollment form and a signature guarantee. The signature guarantee can be included with the letter of instruction. No notarization is usually necessary.

Documents Needed to Change Ownership

After the death of the decedent some states have probate laws requiring proof of payment of any estate or inheritance taxes before they will allow certain property to be transferred to beneficiaries or heirs. If you are a personal representative, you must obtain a *tax waiver* and it must be issued for the value of the property at the date of death. The waiver can be obtained from your state's department of taxation or its local office. Copies of the waiver should be made to distribute if and when necessary, and the original document on the state's official letterhead should be kept available just in case a copy will not do.

Certification of the death of the decedent, known as a *death certificate*, can be provided to heirs by the funeral director or from City Hall or other agencies responsible for keeping local records of vital statistics in your community. This certificate is the legal proof of the decedent's death and copies must be certified by an ink seal or raised stamp.

There are many ways to hold title to property. No one way is best. It would depend on your circumstances and what is appropriate for you and your family. As mentioned, property can be held solely in your name, as community property, and under partnerships, among others. The ways and means of registering and transferring property that would allow for tax savings and provide financial security for other family members has also been discussed here as well as joint ownership of property, which has become a most popular form of transferring property at death and, in addition, avoids the probate process. But there have been challenges by the courts, and larger joint accounts have been vulnerable to oversight by the IRS. A living trust created by you requires a little more work on your part, and you have to pay the cost of preparing a trust document, but a trust can indeed give you greater flexibility than some other methods of ownership and property transfer. You should consult carefully with members of your estate-planning team as to how to own, register, and transfer property and any changes that may be warranted because of changes in your family situation.

11

Life Insurance As an Estate Planning Tool

As we live our lives at work, at home, or at play, many of us are confronted with and exposed to numerous risks that can have a negative impact on ourselves and our family. If these risks turn out to be actual occurrences and we haven't protected ourselves, deep financial and emotional problems can follow. Some risks are so limited in scope and the discomfort or loss so inconsequential that little effort is made to shield us from their possible occurrence. Other risks, however, can have serious consequences. Having insurance is one way to help to protect yourself financially from unpredictable and possibly catastrophic events. Although there are many types of protection, life insurance has been for years, and continues to be, an integral part of one's financial and estate planning. It usually lasts a lifetime, and its lack can have an alarming effect on your spouse and beneficiaries who may not have the money to pay doctors' bills, debts, and death taxes, among other expenses related to your death.

When you purchase life insurance, or someone else does, on your life, it is not intended to be a risk-associated investment that can have a possible appreciation factor, such as shares of stock, perhaps, or corporate bonds that produce current income. Its purpose is to

163

guarantee a certain sum to named beneficiaries if your death is premature and to protect your family from financial exposure. Life insurance is also employed as an estate-planning tool to avoid probate, to reduce or eliminate estate tax liability, and to provide liquidity to the surviving spouse so that postmortem expenses can be paid.

Indeed, a life insurance program should be considered as part of your estate-planning package not because your death is uncertain, but because the *time* of your death is uncertain.

Insurance Proceeds and Estate Planning

Proceeds from an insurance policy that are received by persons specifically named in the policy as beneficiaries will avoid probate. Estate taxes, however, will have to be paid if you, as the decedent, personally held title to the policy at the moment of death. If your *estate* is named as beneficiary of the proceeds of a life insurance policy, the amount when received from the insurance company will become part of your gross estate and be subject to estate tax liability. If the insurance policy, however, is owned by someone other than yourself then the insurance proceeds are not included as part of your estate and are paid promptly to the named beneficiaries. What would happen if there was no beneficiary of record named in the policy but you were the insured? The proceeds would then go to your taxable estate. Additionally, if you name your beneficiaries in your will rather than the insurance policy, then the proceeds would also become part of your taxable estate. Unfortunately, it does not escape probate. When you specifically name your spouse as the beneficiary of an insurance policy that you own, the proceeds can pass tax free as an unlimited marital deduction. Insurance proceeds* can indeed provide estate liquidity, and the financial support to pay for funeral expenses, death taxes, and decedent's debts, among other things. It allows the executor (personal representative) the option of not having to sell nonliquid assets at losses or lower than their value to raise immediate cash.

How can the right kind of insurance planning reduce estate tax liability and also add needed liquidity for estate settlement purposes? If you own life insurance yourself that is titled in your name and you have an estate approaching the $600,000 level, the value of your estate may be pushed above the amount of the lifetime exemption equivalent and subject your estate to substantial estate tax. Of course, as we had mentioned previously, if you name your spouse as unconditional beneficiary of the property, then the proceeds will pass free of tax under the unlimited marital deduction. But qualification for the deduction requires that the spouse also have unrestricted control over any unpaid proceeds. Additionally, any assignment of insurance policies between spouses also avoids not only gift taxes but estate taxes later when the proceeds are paid.

In order to shelter those life insurance proceeds from estate tax you cannot own or control the insurance policy. This means that any "incidents of ownership" on your part would make the cash value of the policy subject to tax. Incidents of ownership are classified as

- The right to surrender or cancel the policy or to change beneficiaries
- The right to pledge the policy for a loan or to obtain a loan from the insurance company against the cash value in the policy

---

*Many people purchase an annuity with insurance proceeds. Annuities are discussed in Chapter 12.

- The ability to assign the policy or to revoke any assignment
- The power to have ownership transferred to someone else

Establishing and retaining ownership of an insurance policy by you can be costly. Have someone else own it. You can do this very simply by gifting a certain sum to those you choose and have them purchase the policy on your life. Under the unified gift and estate tax law you may gift up to $10,000 per year per donee without gift tax but that does not insure that those who receive the gift will want to use the money for insurance premiums rather than purchase perhaps a new car. There can and should be a family understanding that the money used now to pay premiums will lead to a much greater payoff to them when they receive the tax free insurance proceeds at your death.

If you currently hold title to any life insurance policy in your name alone, it might be a good idea to relinquish all rights to it and assign it to someone else, but if you do you may be subject to gift tax. The tax, however, would be nil if it were assigned to your spouse employing the unlimited marital deduction.

The Three-Year Rule

Unless there appears to be a clear and compelling reason to the contrary, assigning your insurance policy to someone else if it is valued near or above the $600,000 tax-free threshold makes good sense. Unfortunately, if you do this and die within three years of the date of assignment, the proceeds would be thrown back into your estate and be subject to estate duties. When it takes place more than three years before death, the proceeds are generally not subject to estate tax. However, if you, as the insured, continue to make premium payments *after* the assignment, you would be subject to *gift* tax to the extent that such payments exceed the $10,000 annual exclusion. I might add that transfers of property other than insurance are not affected by the three-year rule and are excluded from your gross estate for federal tax purposes.

A similar situation can occur if you die within three years of establishing an irrevocable life insurance trust. The proceeds from the insurance policy are included in your taxable estate. This being the case, a clause should be included in your trust instrument that states in effect: "should the grantor die within three years of the establishment of this trust, then the insurance proceeds would go directly to the spouse or into a trust for the surviving spouse's benefit." If this is not done, then the proceeds will revert to your estate and be taxed appropriately.

What is the value of the insurance policy if and when it is assigned to the trust? It is the replacement cost of the policy, that is the amount it would cost to replace the policy under the same terms and conditions as the current policy. Your insurance agent can provide you with this information.

Life Insurance and the Living Trust

Creating a living trust that has a life insurance policy as its primary asset is an advantageous tool in estate planning. It can be established as a revocable or irrevocable living trust. In a revocable insurance trust the insurance proceeds paid at your death can avoid probate costs but have no estate tax savings because the asset, although titled in the name of the revocable trust, continued under your control and ownership as grantor. Because it is a revocable trust and created during your lifetime, you can change your mind and revoke the trust, change beneficiaries, or delete those named in the document and replace them with others. When you die, the trust proceeds are distributed accordingly, either staggered in time of distribution or the beneficiaries can receive all the payments at once.

An advantage of a revocable insurance trust is that it enables you as the current trustee, or one that you name, to provide financial oversight of your affairs, protects the estate and its beneficiaries against possible mismanagement by unsophisticated family members, and acts as a shield against the depletion of your assets. A disadvantage, however, is that it can be an expense to create and administer this trust over a period of years. Another negative, and perhaps more important, is that the value of the trust assets including any insurance proceeds paid to beneficiaries at your death, are subject to estate taxes above the $600,000 or current exemption threshold. This makes the *revocable* insurance living trust a somewhat unattractive tax-saving estate-planning tool.

The Irrevocable Life Insurance Trust

On the other hand, an *irrevocable* trust can be a valuable tax shelter and still remains relatively untouched by Congress. It is among the safest and most effective means of leaving a substantial amount of money to children, spouse, and other beneficiaries free from estate tax liability and probate costs. You, as grantor, however, give up the right to surrender or cancel the policy, change beneficiaries, modify the document, assign it to another, or borrow against the cash value. In fact, once the policy is in force you lose all control over it. If you become divorced and wish to change beneficiaries to reflect the changed situation in your life, it cannot be done. The

legal and tax guidelines are very strict and must be ad-
hered to.

If you wish to use an insurance product as part of your
estate planning it is important that you name an irrevocable trust created by you in which the trust is named specifically as beneficiary of the proceeds. The trust
instrument should be written so that it allows the purchase of, or transfer to the trust, of insurance on your life
as the insured. The trust then becomes the legal owner of
the policy. But you should be very careful not to pay the
insurance premiums personally because if you do you
are, in effect, making gifts to the trust for the benefit of
heirs in the future. This could precipitate tax problems
for you. Why? Because we learned that in order for future
gifts to be free of tax liability, regardless of whether they
fall under the $10,000 per person per donee yearly gift
tax exemption or not, they will be taxed from the *first*
dollar because the donee-beneficiary does not have immediate and complete use of the money. Consequently, if
it is a gift of "future interest" it would have reduced your
lifetime exemption equivalent of $600,000 by the value
of the gift, or, if the exemption is not used for any reason,
the gift amount becomes subject to current tax liability.
You can avoid this prospect, however, by including a
Crummey Provision in the documents and making it
what is commonly referred to as a Crummey trust.

Crummey Trusts

The question of "present" or "future" interest can be resolved by creating an irrevocable insurance trust that
contains a Crummey provision in it. The use of this provision allows you and perhaps other donors to gift up to
$10,000 each directly to the trustee rather than to indi-
vidual beneficiaries. The trustee, however, is then obli-

gated to notify each beneficiary within a stated period, usually thirty days, and generally at the end of the year that the gifts were made. The donee-beneficiaries then have the legal right to collect on the gifts if they so choose and have their immediate use and enjoyment. If any beneficiary decides not to take the gift money, the amount(s) can then be used by the trustee to make the required insurance premiums as instructed. Although the beneficiaries cannot be prevented from taking the money under this provision, the fact is that they have been given the option to do so, which creates a nontaxable gift. The beneficiaries also generally understand that it is in their best long-term interest to allow the money to be used for the payment of premiums upon which they will collect at some future date.

If you wish to have your insurance trust funded with premiums that require a substantial sum, you can choose to use, tax free, all or part of your lifetime exemption equivalent of $600,000 to fund the insurance policy. Not only will this amount be removed from your taxable estate but the trustee can be empowered to purchase a single premium insurance product that can provide a highly leveraged return for spouse and family on receipt of the death benefit. Indeed, an irrevocable trust of this type can add flexibility to your estate plan. It can allow the trustee to have limited discretionary powers to pay insurance proceeds where required at your death, for debts that were incurred and for funeral expenses, among other things. But, in its broader aspects, the irrevocable trust can also formulate and arrange a broad plan of distribution so proceeds can be paid out based on your instructions and guidelines previously placed in the trust document.

Crummey trusts have been used as an estate-planning device for years but their legality has never been fully established. Although, the IRS has not actively challenged their use, it has questioned the grantor's contention that the mere right of the beneficiary to withdraw the funds will constitute an acceptable present interest. Because of this, the grantor must make certain that all beneficiaries be informed periodically of their right to withdraw funds from the trust and that the money is there for that purpose.

Single-Premium Policy vs. One Having Periodic Payments

When a trust is funded with life insurance, the trustee can make arrangements to purchase either a single-premium policy or one having a periodic payment schedule. The single-premium policy will give the trust substantial longer term leveraging characteristics and provide an ultimate death benefit that can amount to three or perhaps four times the original one-time payment if the policy is taken out early enough in the insured's life. This is so because the insurance company receives all of the premium money "up front" and can invest it for themselves immediately. This single-payment option can and should be compared by you or your trustee to the other choice, that is making a succession of payments over a period of years or for the life of the policy. What you elect to do would depend on personal choice, monetary considerations, and also a comparison of illustrations and death-benefit projections provided by your insurance agent. While the single premium reduces the size of your taxable estate immediately by removing an amount equal to the payment, which can be substantial, you are giving up the use of that money that you and/or your spouse may need in the future. You are also allowing the insurance company to invest your money over a long period of years to receive a somewhat higher return——a return you

might be receiving had you not made that single-premium payment. Could you have invested the money
yourself and received a better tax-free return? Maybe.

Those who use the single-payment option seem to
have enough money not to worry about it and would
rather remove the funds currently from their taxable estate and take advantage of part or all of their lifetime exemption equivalent and get it over with by having a fully
paid-up policy. Periodic payments, by comparison, have
short-term leveraging characteristics that are substantial
provided that the insured dies in the early years of the
policy life. Why? Because whoever is paying the premiums would not be required to pay them for too long and
the insurance company would have to pay an early death
benefit. On the other hand, all the money that would
have been used to pay the single premium remains in
your estate and becomes subject to estate taxes and probate. More people would take the more prudent option
and use a periodic payment plan because less money is
required, initially.

Some purchasers of an insurance product will attempt
to compare the tax-free return in the form of a death benefit that the policy produces versus a long-term investment in tax-free bonds. Although insurance is not an
investment per se, you are placing a substantial asset into
a trust for the purpose of providing financial security for
your family and other beneficiaries. Insurance does not
have an exceptionally high value for gift tax purposes
when the policy is purchased with a single premium, but
the leverage is substantial if you consider the amount of
death benefit available soon after purchasing the policy.
It would take many years of successful investing for one
to reach the death benefit level on a tax-free basis with
municipal bonds. Insurance will generally give the trust
a greater net return simply because tax-free bonds do not
provide high enough yields to compete with those non-

taxable returns offered by insurance companies unless the bonds are purchased in your early years and have long-term maturities of twenty-five to thirty-five years that can provide relatively high yields.

The discussion so far should leave little doubt that an irrevocable insurance trust properly constructed can provide economic benefits to you and your family. True, there are legal costs involved in drafting and administering the trust, but if it holds only one or two insurance policies (rather than a portfolio of investment securities) as its prime or only asset, then the management costs can be minimal. You may have an independent corporate trustee, such as a bank or trust company, or a competent individual who is knowledgeable and trustworthy as manager and administrator. The trustee would then make the premium payments, if periodic, and be the owner and beneficiary of the insurance proceeds. This would allow the monies going into the trust at your death to be immediately managed (and later distributed) to those persons named as ultimate beneficiaries with administrative costs or any payment of income or estate taxes to be disbursed by the trustee when required.

One of the concerns that the maker of an irrevocable insurance trust might have, has to do with the protection and care of perhaps a minor child or a beneficiary who is incapacitated. Insurance companies will, in all likelihood, refuse to pay proceeds directly to a beneficiary who cannot handle his or her own affairs and as a result may go to court for the purpose of having it appoint a conservator or guardian. This can mean delays and unprepared for costs. Having an irrevocable trust with a trustee to use insurance proceeds properly and effectively can indeed be very helpful in preventing this.

As noted earlier in the chapter, revocable and irrevocable trusts that are created during the grantor's lifetime are known as living trusts. Forming a *testamentary* trust created as part of your will and not becoming operative until you die is also an option. Here an insurance policy can be purchased while you are alive and held as part of your estate until death. After that, the will is probated and policy proceeds are collected by the trust for the benefit of named beneficiaries. This type of arrangement will allow the proceeds that would ordinarily go to beneficiaries as a lump sum payment at your death to be distributed to them as directed under the terms of your will.

Joint and Survivor Policy

Having an insurance policy that will cover *two* lives instead of just your own can give you greater death benefit leverage because the insurance company doesn't have to pay the death benefit until the second insured dies. We mentioned previously that the surviving spouse can have an estate tax problem when the first spouse attempts to shift money out of his or her taxable estate into that of the survivor. This can create major tax liability later on for the survivor. To plan for this occurrence a joint and survivor policy, otherwise known as "second to die" insurance can be constructed to cover two life expectancies. Its purpose is to pay any estate taxes that are owed after the second spouse dies. It can highly leverage the premium payments either single or yearly and has been thought of as one of the most reasonably priced insurance products you can purchase.

Policy Benefits and Illustrations

When you or your trustee contact an insurance company for information regarding the purchase of a policy, the insurance agent will make an initial presentation of a computerized illustration showing projected policy values and death benefit amounts that your beneficiaries are likely to receive at your death, after receiving some cursory medical information from you as the prospective insured. The amounts are based on the company's analysis of interest or dividends credited to your insurance policy and paid out by the company, on average, over the succeeding period of years.

Most insurance companies will "guarantee" a rate of return of 3.5 to 4.5 percent, but will also offer holders a higher "current rate" that is adjusted periodically to reflect market conditions and to compete for your insurance dollars with other insurance companies. Note that insurance companies invest *your* insurance dollars for their accounts. If they do not receive an adequate rate of return from those and other investments, it can affect the death benefit projected for your beneficiaries. The benefit could be somewhat higher or lower. If lower and you wish to maintain the amount as previously stated, you or your trustee may have to add some additional premium. This is likely to happen, however, only when there is an extended period of low-interest returns available in the market or some catastrophic event occurs to the company.

Insurance Company Disclaimers

To protect themselves from lawsuits by those beneficiaries who were made unhappy by having expectations of a higher death benefit than they received, every insurance company issues a disclaimer shown in each company illustration and the following company disclaimer is from an actual insurance company illustration:

"Illustrated dividends" or interest projected are hypothetical investment results and illustrative only and should not be deemed to be a representation of past or future results. Projected values reflect claim and expense experience of the company and are estimates, not guarantees of future results. Actual investment results and figures shown may be more or less than those shown. Unscheduled increases in additional premium payments are also subject to new underwriting and service fees.

Health Ratings

If an insurance policy is being purchased on your life, the rating that you receive from the company after you have taken a complete physical examination by their representative will have something to do with how much your premiums are. If the company gives you a *substandard* health rating, you fall into a group of insureds that the company says has increased risks of an early death and consequently the owner of the policy will have to pay more than perhaps some other insureds to sustain an equal amount of death benefit and length of coverage. One who receives, on the other hand, a *preferred* rating and falls into a group of lower actuarial risk to the company will pay somewhat less. The *standard* rating is situated between the two. Any insurance company, in assessing ratings and mortality charges to clients, will take into account in particular the medical history and smoking habits of the insured before issuing the policy coverage.

How Safe Is Your Insurance Company?

Insurance companies can indeed have financial difficulties, especially in periods of reduced economic activity in the country. Several have failed in the last decade because of problems mainly related to investments in real estate. Insurance carriers can also run into financial difficulty when they have several of the following occur: (a) higher than projected mortality costs, (b) excessive claims, (c) too many policy holders cashing in on policies, (d) a catastrophic natural event that reduces its economic resources, (e) poor investment performance, (f) a lower level of interest rate receipts on investment, (g) higher than expected operating expenses, (h) a constant increasing number of underperforming loans, (i) and, of course, a loss in the value of real estate investments. All of these elements can have some effect on the rate of return that the company will pay periodically on its policies. If the company does well and their economic resources increase and their investments are profitable, then interest or dividends that the company pay to policyholders will also be increased. If the company is not profitable, then you may be in a position of some risk as a policyholder.

What to Look for When Choosing an Insurance Company

Solvency is the measure of assets to liabilities, which is the ability of a company to meet its obligations.

Capital Surplus is like policy reserves and indicates the amount of cushion that the company has backing its obligations to policyholders. The larger the reserves the better.

Capital Ratio represents the amount of reserves relative to assets that the company maintains to protect against loss or changes in assets due to economic conditions. A ratio higher than average indicates a stronger capital position.

In addition to solvency, capital surplus, and capital

ratio, you need to know what percentage of the total portfolio of the insurance company are below-investment-
grade bonds, the percentage of problem mortgages, and
how many other bad loans the company is carrying on its
books. Also, what has been the company's net yield on
investment over the past ten years, and what have they
paid to policyholders? You are not going to be able to get
answers to all these questions from the insurance agent
or from your own research, but whatever information
you can accumulate will help. It is a very difficult area to
research and make valid comparisons, and you may want
to consult an independent insurance agent or adviser to
help you.

Insurance companies—unlike commercial banks, savings banks, and savings and loan associations— are not
federally regulated currently nor are individual insurance companies insured by any agency of the U.S. government. Individual states do supervise the activities of
insurance companies but are limited by law as to what
they can do. After all, these are private corporations. Insurance companies, however, do help each other when
financial troubles arise and individually contribute to a
special fund that is employed collectively for financial
emergencies. Obviously, if one or two insurance companies go bankrupt, the entire industry is affected and people shy away from buying policies. Although the
emergency funds can be of help to those policyholders
who were unfortunate enough to own policies with the
company in financial difficulty, one cannot count on
such funds. Therefore, if you have insurance in mind,
deal only with the very strongest companies and those
assigned the highest ratings by at least two rating services.

For information on the financial soundness of individual insurance companies, it is prudent to research the
rating services that are published periodically, offering

monthly and quarterly evaluations of the company status of each. Among the services are *Weiss Ratings Inc.,* Palm Beach Gardens, Fla., (407) 627-3300; *A.M. Best and Co.,* Oedvick, N.J., (900) 420-0400; *Standard and Poor's,* Insurance Rating Service, New York, N.Y., (212) 208-1527; *Duff and Phelps Inc.,* Chicago, Ill., (312) 368-3157; and *Moody's Investor Services Inc.,* New York, N.Y., (212) 553-0377.

Although there are slight variations on how the rating services describe their evaluations, all of them consider a **Triple-A (AAA)** company as having an extremely strong capacity to meet contractual policy obligations and an exceptional, or the highest, claims-paying ability; a **Double-A (AA)** company as having a very strong capacity to meet contractual policy obligations and an excellent, or relied-on high, claims-paying ability; and an **A** company as having a strong capacity to meet contractual obligations and a good, or a high, claims-paying ability.

A **Triple-B (BBB)** company is adequate, a **Double-B (BB)** company is below average, and a **B** company is questionable.

Life insurance can be a liquid source of funds for your estate, your spouse, and your family. Try to balance the dollar amount of premiums you pay (if you don't have a paid-up policy) with your needs that occur on a continuing basis. Will one of your policies be used for lifetime retirement income rather than as an ultimate death benefit? Will a lifetime pay out to your surviving spouse after your death be enough? This will require an assessment of your current and future needs. Review your policy with your agent to make sure of this.

Having an appropriate insurance program not only goes a long way in protecting your family but, when properly constructed, it may be used for advantageous tax planning by helping to pay estate taxes with death benefit proceeds which may be worth far in excess of the policy's cash values. You must, however, be certain not to own the policy yourself or the proceeds will be subject to estate tax at your death. With this in mind, you should consider the use of an irrevocable single-premium life insurance trust, an excellent planning tool that is especially attractive if you have a medium to large estate because it reduces the size of the estate, can protect a leveraged death benefit from taxes, and can increase assets outside your estate to pay for administrative probate and other estate-related expenses.

12

The Transfer and Distribution of Retirement Assets

If you are about to retire, you will be faced with many decisions, both personal and financial. One of the more difficult questions that must be resolved has to do with the level and quality of life you and your spouse expect to maintain after retirement. Another is how much in spendable funds will be available to preserve the lifestyle to which both of you have become accustomed after your weekly paychecks stop? Most potential retirees tend to focus on the pleasant things they will be doing when retirement comes: the freedom from work, no schedules to contend with, and time to play golf and tennis, to draw and paint, to travel and do anything else they wish. But sooner or later one question must be addressed: Where will the money come from and how much will there be? Yes, you were a participant in a retirement program and, of course, there *is* social security. Indeed, your plan's benefits may be very generous and there may be little reason to be concerned, but many plans are not generous and provide only minimal benefits to fulfill the financial requirements of you and your spouse. We, as a nation, are living longer and are much more active later in life than prior generations were. Older Americans are now in better health and have a much wider choice of leisure time activities than their predecessors had. If you haven't been a participant in a qualified retirement plan, such as a corporate pension or profit-saving plan, a Keogh, or a public retirement program, it may be difficult to initiate and maintain a particular standard of living that you once envisaged.

No one can dispute the importance of starting a retirement program early in life. Tax-deferral over a long period of years, regardless of the illiquidity of the program, should provide a formidable fund to achieve your retirement goals. Time was a friend and an ally to you and your family and if you have not done so until now, there is still time to develop some useful plan as long as your expectations are reasonable regarding the amount of income the program can generate and make available to you and your spouse during retirement. This chapter is not directed, however, toward the *pre*-retirement asset-buildup phase of financial planning, but is more specifically focused on *establishing a linkage between retirement and estate planning* and how your current decision making can impact the financial well-being of you, your spouse, and possible beneficiaries.

At this point in your life you are likely to have some idea as to how much monthly income you will be receiving as periodic payments from one, two, or possibly more retirement, annuity, or investment programs. In addition to checking on your social security benefits, if you haven't already done so, you might visit with your company-plan administrator who can tell you what you can expect to receive from your retirement plan(s). The option as to investment objectives that you chose twenty or thirty years ago when you made the selection has resulted in a certain outcome. If, for instance, you decided on an investment program of growth-stock rather than an income-oriented plan, your periodic benefit payment is probably appreciably greater. Additionally, it might also be a good time to see who are shown as beneficiaries of your plan and if you need to make any changes.

If your employer did not have a 401(k) retirement program, and instead you are a participant in an IRA, a Keogh, or an annuity program, you must consider these programs in your estate planning because they often have funds available to beneficiaries as part of your estate distribution. For instance, monies left in an IRA go to a named beneficiary without probate but are included in your gross estate for death tax purposes. Other retirement accounts, or assets such as an insurance policy, have designated beneficiaries written into the account, and those funds go directly to the beneficiaries. A will generally cannot dictate in these cases, who the beneficiary of the plan is. If, however, the plan does name your estate as beneficiary, then the intentions of the testator through the will document should state who is to receive the proceeds, which are then distributed to that person(s) as the will provides.

Some Sources of Retirement Income

1. Social security
2. Qualified Plans:
    Corporate salary deferral 401 (k) plans
    Corporate thrift plans
    Employee stock ownership plans (ESOP)
    Government pension plans
    Keogh plan
    Simplified employee pension plan (SEP)
    Tax-sheltered annuity 403 (b) plan
3. Annuities and IRA's
4. Personal investing and management, bank accounts, certificates of deposit (CDs), stocks, bonds, mutual funds, etc.

Social Security

The most extensive and well-known retirement plan is social security. It provides payments to covered wage earners and others who are classified in various categories as family survivors. Any retirement planning should have been built around this basic program. Some people believe that the social security system will be bankrupt by the time they are to receive their benefits, but at *this* time the social security trust fund appears to be alive and well. As a result, you can reasonably count on a regular although modest amount each month to help support you and your spouse during retirement. Whether or not the present system will remain as it is presently constructed is an open question.

Because of longer life expectancies, full retirement age—currently sixty-five—will be increased gradually until it reaches age 67. This change begins in the year 2000, and it affects people born in 1938 and later. You can start your benefits as early as age sixty-two, but at a reduced level. What you will receive during retirement is calculated by the social security administration according to a formula based on contributions you have made over your working years and the age at which you plan to retire. To obtain an estimate of the social security benefit that you will receive after retirement you can request a "Personal Earnings and Benefit Estimate Statement" from the Social Security Administration on form SSA 7004. (telephone: 1-800-772-1213). Currently 85 percent of social security benefits can be subject to income tax for those whose income has reached a particular level. Social security currently replaces 37–39 percent of preretirement income, and each year its payments are reduced as your earnings climb above a certain amount. If you were fortunate enough to be in a qualified retirement program and you contributed over an extended period of time, you could be in the 60 + percent pool of potential retirees who can currently replace approximately 40–42 percent of their preretirement income.

But if you did not plan for your retirement and you are in that unenviable position of not believing you will have enough income to maintain a decent standard of living, you can continue to work and earn up to a certain limit and still receive your social security checks. These limits increase each year as average wages increase. If your earnings go over the legal limit some or all of your benefits will be offset by your earnings. For instance; if you are under 65, $1 in benefits will be deducted for each $2 in earnings above the limit. If you are 65 through 69, $1 in benefits will be deducted for each $3 in earnings above the limit.

Earnings received during or after the month you reach 70 will not affect your social security benefits, but if another family member receives benefits on your social security record, total family benefits can be affected by your earnings.*

Qualified Retirement Plans

A qualified plan is one that meets specific Internal Revenue Code conditions and guidelines regarding benefits offered, certain tax-reporting requirements, and criteria for participant eligibility. A qualified plan has tax advantages not only for the employer but also for the employee.

---

*Social security benefits are reduced when recipients earn over a certain amount each year. Under current law, the earnings ceiling will continue to rise from $13,500 in 1997 to $14,500 in 1998, to $15,500 in 1999, to $17,000 in the year 2000, to $25,000 in 2001, and to $30,000 in the year 2002. After 2002, the earnings limit will continue to be adjusted annually to reflect average wage increases.

Many sponsors of 401 (k) or 403 (b) plans will partially or fully match the plan contributions that you made in the past on a pretax basis. You were allowed to defer any then-current taxation on whatever amounts you placed into the plan and to pay less in overall taxes on other income you received. Earnings that were, or are now, being accumulated in the plan are set aside and are not taxed until paid out to you or your beneficiaries. In addition, the employer you worked for or the one you are currently employed by is permitted to receive an immediate tax deduction on contributions that the firm makes to the plan. Also, a qualified plan is required to be formalized not only for contributions but also for distributions. In addition, the plan generally is not allowed to discriminate in favor any particular group of employees, such as higher paid executives. In spite of this Congress passed in the latter part of 1996 what we shall call the "tax reform act of 1996"* that actually *eased* rules that forbade 401 (k) and other pension plans from favoring highly paid employees.

The amount of pay out you receive will depend on several factors including the length of time you were employed by the company or institution and your salary level expressed as "an average over a period of time, generally the last five years." This average is then translated into a specific amount of retirement credit(s) that will determine your dollar pay out, with any inflation adjustments or cost of living increases to be factored in. If you decide to take a lump-sum payment, there may be taxes to pay. You can choose, however, to keep the amount of the distribution in a tax-sheltered plan and not pay the tax on a current basis. For many people, maintaining the

---

*The tax reform act of 1996 really comprises three individual bills passed by Congress and known as the Small Business Protection Act, the Health Insurance Portability and Accountability Act, and the Personal Responsibility and Work Opportunity Reconciliation Act.

tax-deferred program makes more sense unless there are compelling personal reasons why you should not do so. What you decide can have an impact on your financial security and that of your family.

Distributions and Rollovers

Should you take a lump-sum distribution from an employer-sponsored retirement plan? This is an important decision for you, and you have several options:

1. Taking a lump sum payment and rolling it over into an IRA account within sixty days is called an *indirect rollover.*
2. Instructing your employer to send the money to your IRA institution is a *direct trustee-to-trustee rollover.* In this case you do not take possession of the funds. It is important that you decide what you want to do several months before the target date so you can give your employer enough time to make arrangements to transfer your account into another qualified tax-deferred plan and avoid any possible penalties.
3. Taking your distribution and paying whatever taxes are required, would give you immediate and unrestricted use of the funds. The drawback of the large tax liability would appear to outweigh this advantage unless you absolutely had to have the money for good and sufficient reasons.
4. Leaving the money in your employer's current tax-deferred plan or in a new one being offered.
5. Requesting that a certain amount in your account be employed to purchase a single-premium annuity contract under an IRA. Although often done, such an action may not be a good idea because the rate

of return under an IRA investment is already tax-deferred so you are just adding another layer of expenses in the form of mortality charges and other additional administrative costs.

6. Continuing to work when you are older than seventy-and-one-half and continuing to defer income (providing you own less than 5 percent or more of the company). This option became possible in 1997 when Congress repealed the requirement that pension plan distributions from company-sponsored and other qualified plans, such as Keoghs, must begin at age seventy and one-half *even if the employee is still working.*

Penalties and Tax Considerations

Most likely, you will have to pay income taxes on the receipt of all retirement benefits, except after-tax contributions that you made into a qualified plan. Future earnings, if not under a tax-deferred umbrella, will be taxed in the year they are received. In addition, if you receive a total of more than $160,000 from your retirement plan (in 1997),* or a lump sum in excess of $800,000 (in 1997),* then a 15 percent excess distribution tax would be imposed. A provision, however, in the tax reform act of 1996 repeals this tax penalty temporarily until December 31, 1999. As an employee who receives a lump-sum distribution from a qualified plan as a result of a plan dissolution, disability, or termination of employment, you are eligible to rollover the funds in your retirement account that represent all pretax contributions made by you, all company contributions, and all investment income and earnings accrued in your account. Any voluntary, nonde-

---

*These amounts are indexed every year for inflation.

ductible contributions you made to your employee plan are not eligible for rollover treatment.

In doing a *direct rollover* of the retirement plan distribution, your retirement plan payment should state clearly that it is made payable to the new plan and indicate in writing on the check that it is *for the benefit of* (FBO) your name, any applicable account number, and your social security number. Here, you have not in fact received the money. The check was merely a conduit to the new tax-deferred plan. When the distribution takes place, no tax will be assessed. If you do a partial rollover, however, you will be taxed on what remains. Special tax treatment is forfeited on a partial rollover. The IRS is unforgiving if you don't meet the sixty-day deposit deadline for the *indirect rollover*. Your employer can draw a check to you, but you must watch the calendar and use the money for no more than sixty days before rolling it into the IRA account. The tax penalty far outweighs any advantages.

Under 1993 legislation, mandatory withholding rules were passed that can affect you adversely *if you do not choose a direct rollover* of retirement funds. Before you receive your lump sum withdrawal, the government will withhold from a variety of employer-sponsored retirement plans including 401 (K) plans, profit sharing, and Keogh plans as well as state and county retirement programs, 20 percent of your retirement check.

So, to protect *all* of your personal retirement money from taxes and possible penalties, do a direct rollover or you may have to fund the entire amount withheld from out of your own pocket. As you evaluate the options, and after you have talked to your company benefits specialist, you may decide to take your distribution in equal installments, which are referred to as *periodic payments*. This money is taxed only as you receive it. Periodic payments do pose a problem, however, as you can lose the option of transferring money into another employer plan or into an IRA rollover and, in addition, you can be subject to a 10 percent penalty if you don't follow a scheduled five-year program, or until you reach fifty-nine and one-half years of age. Two publications that I would highly recommend that summarize special tax treatments are IRS Publication #575, "Pensions and Annuity Income," and #590 on IRA rules.

To be sure, pitfalls do exist involving distributions, and one of your main concerns should be to eliminate the possibility that any penalties or taxes will be assessed against you. You can be penalized by the IRS for premature distributions, excess distributions, in addition to court ordered distributions, and you can be subject to other rules, regulations, and exceptions that may leave you vulnerable if you are not careful. That 10 percent penalty tax for *early* distributions from qualified plans equals 10 percent of that portion that is includable in your gross income by reason of the distributions. It will not apply, however, if the distribution is made

- because you as the employee become disabled,
- after age fifty-nine and one-half,
- to a beneficiary of your estate after your death,
- as part of a series of equal distributions during your life,
- for you exclusively or for both you and your beneficiary.

If you rollover the distribution you can avoid tax liability. Also, there is no tax on withdrawal of nondeductible contributions.

A more traditional plan, such as the *corporate thrift plan*, is also a matching plan, but contributions are not tax deductible. You, as an employee, are required to pay income tax on the contributions you make or that were made for you while you were working on a current basis. Earnings on investments, however, are tax deferred but taxed on distribution. Principal pay out is not taxed because you paid your taxes when you made contributions to the plan.

If you are the one who has the legal right to receive the retirement benefits, from whatever qualified plan, then you are under the obligation not only to determine whether or not the benefits are taxable, but also to pay any tax liability. Here, your best bet is to check with the employee benefits specialist at your current or previous employer for all necessary information. Compensation packages from retirement programs vary so much that it would be ludicrous to attempt to cover all of the possibilities here. As a married person, when filing a joint return, you must combine any retirement benefits in your computations if any of the benefits are deemed to be taxable. As one owning an annuity, for example, if you paid a portion of the cost of that annuity, you would not be taxed on the part of the annuity pay out you receive that represents a return of capital. The rest is taxable. The cost, that is, your investment in the plan, includes the total amount you paid into the plan including any amount your employer paid that you were required to report as income and paid taxes on. From the total cost paid by you, you must subtract any refunds on premiums, rebate of dividends, unrepaid loans or any tax-free amounts received before the later of either the annuity starting date or the date you received your first annuity pay out.

Form Filing for Distributions

You must complete IRS *Form 8606* if your distribution was from an IRA that contained nondeductible contributions. The form will help you determine how much of your distribution is taxable and what portion is not. If you take a premature distribution, IRS *Form 5229* must be filed even when the distribution involves the disability or death of the account holder. This form can also be used for excess distributions, excess contributions, and insufficient withdrawals. All distributions, including rollovers, must be reported on a IRS *Form 1040* or *1040A*. If you did not rollover an amount and it was kept by you, it is taxable, except for nondeductible after-tax contributions. On the other hand, payments made to you from profit-sharing plans, pensions, annuities, IRAs, insurance contracts and other retirement plans are reported to the IRS and to you on *Form 1099-R*. The information contained in the form describes, among other things, the dollar amount of distributions received from the payer and the taxable amount for which you are responsible.

Making Your Tax Less Severe

For those of you that would like to take a lump-sum distribution in a particular year and not be fully taxed in that year, *ten year forward averaging* can be part of the solution to make the one-time tax less severe. Forward averaging allows the taxpayer special tax treatment under current law on the receipt of a lump-sum distribution from a qualified retirement program. It is a once-in-a-lifetime election that permits you to complete the payment of tax owed on a distribution as if you have received it in equal amounts over a ten-year election period. You pay your total tax liability in the year the money is received but at a much lower rate. Without the averaging option, the receipt during the completion of the ten-year period of the income distribution would fall under ordinary tax rates. If you made *after tax* contributions to your plan, however, they are not included in the averaging calculations.

You are eligible for forward averaging if

- You are at least fifty-nine and one-half years old and were born prior to January 1, 1936.
- Your distribution is being paid to you because you are permanently disabled if self-employed.
- You have terminated your employment.
- Your distribution is the entire amount that is due you from all similar qualified plans and paid to you within one tax year by the same employer.
- You are the beneficiary of the plan.
- The plan was terminated.
- You were a participant in a qualified company retirement plan, a Keogh, or a 403(b) plan for at least five years.

If you are one who may receive a large lump-sum distribution from your retirement plan you may be disappointed and frustrated to learn that the Tax Act of 1996 has repealed your right to use five-year forward averaging. As a matter of fact, it will be completely phased out and its use disallowed after December 31, 1999. You may, however, continue to employ ten-year averaging just discussed, as a one-time election. *IRS Form 4972* is for computing the tax, but the taxable liability is reported on IRS Form 1040.

IRAs

As a basic long-term savings plan, individual retirement accounts (IRAs) were created in this country for the exclusive benefit of an individual and that person's beneficiaries. It allows you to defer federal income taxes on the amount invested and on the income earned in the account. Retirees who work and earn money are permitted to continue making contributions to an IRA account up to the year in which they attain seventy and one-half years. If you, as a retiree, decide to withdraw funds from an IRA, how much you remove from the account is based to a large extent on personal considerations. However, as money is withdrawn from your account during your retirement years, the total assets that had been accumulated as earned income, including any capital gains attributed to those assets, are all taxed at ordinary income tax rates. You cannot take advantage of any reduced long-term capital gain tax rates or special tax treatment under ten-year income averaging rules. The loss of these options, however, should not diminish the attractiveness of IRAs as a retirement and savings vehicle.*

If you or your spouse continue to be employed, you might like to know that the amount of deferral in an IRA account was broadened by the passage of the tax reform act of 1996, giving a worker's nonworking spouse the opportunity to make a full $2,000 contribution to an IRA. Prior to 1997, couples with only one worker were limited to contributions totaling $2,250, that is, $2,000 for the worker and $250 for the nonworking spouse. The law, however, does not change the limits on deductibility of contributions. It remains the same as prior to January 1, 1997.

If you have an IRA, you must begin to receive periodic distributions from your IRA account by April 1 of the year following the one in which you reach the age of seventy and one-half years or a penalty will be assessed. From that point, withdrawals are based not only on the

---

*The 1996 tax reform act now permits penalty-free early withdrawals from an existing IRA account to pay for medical expenses that exceed 7.5 percent of your adjusted gross income (AGI).

total value of funds in your account, but on your age and life expectancy or on the combined life expectancy of you and your spouse or designated beneficiary, as derived from current official mortality tables.

Beneficial Interests

Retirement plans generally contain clauses that allow the plan to continue to provide benefits to the survivor, the children, and other beneficiaries after the death of the first spouse. Benefits such as these are known beneficial interests and can provide certain options for those named in the plan. For instance, a wife having a beneficial interest can have the option of receiving a lower benefit while she remains alive, in order that the husband shall receive the same continuing or higher benefit until his death.

Benefits, in most cases, have to be applied for, generally by the executor (personal representative) of the estate. If you, as the decedent, were a veteran of the armed forces or were under the Railroad Retirement Act, for example, proper application must be made in order to receive benefits. When you are made the beneficiary of a qualified retirement plan, your spouse at his or her death would receive the unlimited marital deduction on the value of the property left to you. The proceeds, however, at the time of receipt, are subject to income tax liability because had your spouse lived to receive the retirement benefits a tax would have had to be paid on the proceeds. In addition, as a beneficiary of a deceased employee, you may elect special averaging treatment for a qualifying lump-sum distribution received from an employee's death even though the deceased employee was in the plan for less than the five-year minimum.

Retirement assets having designated beneficiaries will

escape the probate process, but if no beneficiary or beneficiaries are named, the proceeds of your retirement plan
after your death will go back into your estate and be subject to tax. Assets, such as IRAs, pension and profit-sharing plans, Keoghs, and so forth, all have provisions to
name designated beneficiaries. The surviving spouse
must, however, under current law be the primary beneficiary and have directly inherited the assets. In this way,
the spouse can either pay income tax liability upon receiving the distribution or postpone the payment of taxes
by the use of a rollover.

Using a Trust

You can also name an existing trust or create a new one
as beneficiary of a retirement account. Some estate planners do this, but there can be the disadvantage of it preventing your spouse from rolling over a retirement asset
or assets for five years under current law. A trust is advantageous, however, when a primary beneficiary is
ruled incompetent at about the time of grantor's death.
When this occurs, the proceeds from the distribution go
into the trust with the successor trustee taking over if the
grantor had been the trustee.

Suppose the named beneficiary of your retirement
plans dies at essentially the same time as you do. The
court may have difficulty in deciding who then receives
the proceeds. It would be resolved eventually, but the un-
certainty can be avoided if a trust agreement is in place
where the contingent trustee named in the document
would assume control of the assets after your death. If
you have accumulated a great deal of money in your IRA
account, you might also establish an A-B trust to reduce
the tax burden on your beneficiaries. Under this trust arrangement, your spouse can have the lifetime rights to

the trust income, then after the surviving spouse dies, the trust assets are transferred to the beneficiaries, bypassing the surviving spouse's estate.

Annuities

After you have taken into account social security, your pension or profit-sharing plan, and perhaps an IRA or a Keogh, you certainly can consider additional investing in an annuity as another way to save money for your later retirement years. Earnings that accumulate under an annuity grow tax deferred and are very similar to other retirement programs. Annuities differ because contributions to them are not deductible but, by the same token, there is no limit on what you can invest. If and when you decide to purchase an annuity, your agreement with an insurance company provides that you give them a specific amount of money or make periodic contributions, and the company agrees to pay you income for a certain number of years or for the rest of your life. Payments to you and your spouse can begin at some future date or immediately. These commercial annuities may have been purchased from a stock brokerage firm or from some other source, but are issued by insurance companies.

The two basic types of annuities are fixed and variable-rate annuities. A *fixed annuity* is one in which the insurance company credits you with a stated fixed interest rate, which is applicable for a period of time and consistent with, but not necessarily the same as, what other insurance companies are paying. This rate can be adjusted when the board of directors of the insurance company decides, depending on the general level of interest rates currently in the marketplace, to make a change in the pay out. *Variable annuities*, on the other hand, have more investment risk but may be appealing to the more venturesome. Here, the money goes into a diversified portfolio of investments that can include stocks, bonds, and other securities. Your rate of return is tied directly to the performance of those investments in the insurance company portfolio.

Variable annuities are purchased by those who seek tax-deferred capital appreciation and accumulation of investment funds and current or future income for themselves and their spouse. The monies received later on from the insurance company are essentially an installment return of your initial investment in addition to any subsequent investments made, plus accrued interest income and/or appreciation received. Expenses related to the purchase, administration, and maintenance of an annuity are charged by the insurance company and indirectly reduce the rate of return to you, in part, because of the life insurance component in the annuity contract.

If you began an annuity program years ago, you probably have a substantial accumulation of funds in your account. Indeed, your original premium payments have been earning interest or dividends for years and you are now in the preretirement or postretirement period and you have to consider what to do. The options that you have are related to the type of contract you originally purchased, but, in general, you are permitted to take a partial withdrawal if you need the money for emergencies but do not want to surrender the contract. Usually you can take out 10 percent of the annuity contract value once each year free of any charges. If, however, you wish to surrender the policy for whatever reason and make a full withdrawal, a surrender charge may be imposed depending upon the company and the insurance contract.

At some later date, you will have to decide whether or not you wish to accept a lump-sum payment and reinvest it yourself or receive annuity payments for a period or for your life and perhaps for the life of your spouse. If you take the lump sum, you will have greater flexibility in investing the principal, although the investing may be a responsibility that you don't need or want. If you go with an annuity with a fixed return, at least you can count on what the company will provide. An annuity with a variable component may give you a greater total return but has added risks.

The basic principle in annuities is that you will not outlive the payments the insurance company makes to you under the annuity contract. As a matter of fact, you may have purchased a *joint and survivor annuity* that pays your income during your life and then when you die, the income stream continues for the rest of your spouse's life. Or an annuity can be purchased for a *period certain* in which income payments are guaranteed for a specific period of time, say ten or twenty years, instead of for life. In addition, your separate life insurance can be part of your retirement income. If you have an annuity option for the pay out of cash values as part of your insurance contract, then you can convert to an annuity and receive income for the rest of your life if you choose.

It might be wise to consider the purchase of a commercial annuity but only after you have reduced or totally eliminated your ability to employ your savings and contribute to an existing 401(K), 403(b) or Keogh. Qualified plans permit contributions on a tax deductible basis, which allows your monies in the account to compound at a much faster rate than having them build up merely tax deferred.

There are also estate tax considerations having to do with annuities. As was stated in a previous chapter an annuity is part of the estate of the decedent. Indeed, the amount included in your gross estate is its current value based on contributions made by you, the decedent, or your employer over time, provided that

1. you are entitled to receive annuity payments, and
2. a beneficiary is stated and is entitled to receive benefits under the annuity contract after your death, and
3. the annuity is paid for under or arising from a formal agreement or contract.

Some people, after the death of a spouse, use their life insurance proceeds to purchase an annuity. Then, the payments received are taxed as annuity income. IRS Publication #939 covers pension and annuity income for those brave enough to read it.

Projecting Valuations

The ultimate value of your retirement accounts and other investments currently depends to a great extent on how well the money was managed over the years. You may have agreed to a fixed return in your retirement plan or to more of a variable investment component in which risks are somewhat greater. Employers have, over the years, attempted to shift the investment risks to the employee even though most will guarantee a minimal level of retirement benefits in their benefit package. If you are not sure of your account's current value, you can ask your employee benefits department to determine what your benefits would be if you retired now. Also, be sure to know what your tax liabilities would be if you considered taking a distribution at a specific age as opposed to working perhaps a few more years. You may get an offer from your employer to consider taking early retirement in exchange for a tempting package of incentives, which may mean that you will have additional monies to add to your existing personal investment and reinvestment programs. But before we discuss that, it is important to examine what your standard of living requirements shall be or currently are and what you and your spouse will need in protected dollars to cover your total expenses now and into the future. You should add approximately 5 percent per year to compensate for the loss of purchasing power because of inflation. Also,

1. Do your best in determining what your current available income is and what it will be from (a) all your qualified plans, (b) your work income if you continue to be employed, (c) your social security, investments, savings, possible inheritances, etc.
2. Identify the types of investments and/or insurance strategy that you feel is appropriate for you and your family.
3. Develop the kind of diversified investment program with available monies that will attempt to meet your financial goals.
4. Use estate-planning tools and tax-saving measures to maintain and increase your retirement income.
5. Employ the inventory income worksheet (below) that will give you a picture of your gross income each year.

If you have been serious in your outlook and diligent in your approach to retirement income planning and personal tax-deferred investing, you should have sufficient sums to work with. When you are no longer working, your investments can produce additional income to at least help you maintain an acceptable standard of living. Of course, nothing in life is certain and many retired people who thought they would "have enough" now realize that it wasn't sufficient to compensate for the loss of purchasing power through the inflationary cycle of the recent past. No one knows whether that cycle will continue.

Projecting the total value of your investments and rely-
ing on those figures for retirement income sometime in
the future can indeed be foolhardy. But, if you cannot
predict with any degree of certainty those amounts, you
can at least get a ball-park figure in spite of the uncertain-
ties surrounding the level of interest rates and inflation.
An aid that is employed by many and frequently used
by professionals to help somewhat in projecting future
valuations is called *"the Rule of Seventy-two."* Although
not exact, it can effectively give you the time it takes to
double the value of your assets. The rule does not take
into account any tax liability, but starts with the number
72 and divides it by an assumed rate of growth; the result
is the length of time that will be required for the value of
your assets to double.

For example, if your net worth, through inflation and
investment savings is growing at the rate of 7.2 percent,
which, when divided into the number 72, shows it will
take ten years to double in value. The rule can be employed to help determine your average annual rate of
gain. If, for example, you purchased a stock ten years ago
for $20 per share and its value doubled so currently it
is worth $40 per share, then you can determine that the
average annual rate of gain is 7.2 percent (72 ÷ 10 =
7.2 percent) achieved over ten years. If your money were
increasing at an 8 percent rate instead of 7.2 percent, it
would take only nine years to double and, if the rate of
increase were 9 percent, eight years would be sufficient
for it to double. If the net worth of your investment is
$400,000 when you are age fifty-five, and you invest it in
federally tax-exempt securities at a 6 percent return, it
will take twelve years (and you will be sixty-seven) for it
to double in value to $800,000, if your state does not have
state income tax.

How much money do you need to invest in order to
receive a certain return later during your retirement pe-

riod and beyond? Table 12.1 below will give you some idea how much you must invest initially at a 6 percent or 7 percent return to receive a particular level of income. This projection does not take into account any federal or state tax liability required to be paid on a yearly basis. If these amounts were invested in tax-exempt securities and you were domiciled in a state in which there was no state income tax (such as Florida currently, among others), no adjustment for tax liability would have to be made. Also, no adjustments for inflation are considered in these computations. Say, for example, you sold your large home that you no longer needed and are now renting a small apartment. After the payment of capital gains tax, if any, expenses, fees, etc., connected with the sale of your residence, you receive a net amount of $256,379. If you took this amount and purchased tax free municipal bonds of the state in which you are presently domiciled and the bonds paid a 7 percent average annual return, you would receive an annual income of $22,000 for twenty-five years. After the first year, for instance, $17,946 would be tax-free income to you that would be

TABLE 12.1
Amount of Investment Required to Produce Various Annual Incomes, from $10,000 to $34,000

INVESTMENT at ANNUAL RATE of		ANNUAL INCOME PRODUCED (Before Taxes)
6%	7%	
$127,834	$116,536	$10,000
178,968	163,150	14,000
230,100	209,764	18,000
281,234	256,379	22,000
332,368	302,993	26,000
383,502	349,607	30,000
434,636	396,222	34,000

added to your total investment. The rest would be a return of capital. However, $22,000 would be removed and available as income to you and your spouse for that year.

Figure 12.1 (see next page) is a worksheet for compiling your yearly gross income inventory. Using it will give you a good estimate of what your year's income can be.

FDIC Insurance Coverage for Retirement Accounts

The general rule for deposits at a bank belonging to a *pension or profit-sharing plan* is that each beneficiary's ascertainable interest in a deposit account, as opposed to the entire deposit by the fund, is insured up to $100,000. This is called "pass-through" insurance and is permitted if the deposit account records disclose that the depositor, in this case the trustee or the retirement plan itself, holds the funds in a fiduciary capacity. Insurance coverage, however, for other retirement programs is somewhat different. Prior to December 19, 1993, IRAs and Keogh funds deposited in the bank were insured separately from each other and from all other funds of the depositor. But now funds will still be separately insured from any nonretirement funds that the depositor may have at the same institution, but IRAs and Keoghs will be added together and the combined total cannot be insured for more than a Federal Deposit Insurance Corporation (FDIC) maximum of $100,000. In addition, under current aggregation rules certain self-directed retirement plans, including deferred compensation plans established by state and local governments, also may fall under 1993 rules but may be eligible for pass-through insurance. See your plan administrator to determine if you qualify.

While making your retirement plans and considering what assets you have that you can draw on for retirement income, keep in mind those whom you name as benefi-

Source of Income	Amount in Your Name	Amount in Spouse's Name	Amount in Joint Names
Social Security			
Bank Accounts (U.S. Savings Bonds)			
Money Market Account			
Mutual Funds			
Stock Brokerage (Securities Held in Street Name)			
Securities Held by You (registered in owner's name)			
Real Estate			
Annuities and Insurance Commercial and Private			
Corporate Retirement Plan			
IRA/Keogh			
SEP			
Government or Public Retirement (Civil Service, Military, Teacher)			
Trusts			
Income from Loans			
Miscellaneous (including secure inheritances)			
TOTALS			

Figure 12.1   Yearly Gross Income Inventory Worksheet

ciaries of your accumulating property. If there is no record of a beneficiary or beneficiaries on your original
plan account application, then the proceeds from your
pension, profit-sharing plan, your IRA, Keogh, or other
qualified plan will be paid to your estate and be subject
to estate tax. Having named a designated beneficiary not
only allows your estate to escape probate costs, but that
named individual will take precedence over those
named in a trust or under a will. The only way that a
will can authorize retirement plan proceeds to go to a
particular person is if your *estate* was named as beneficiary of the plan; then the will would distribute the retirement asset accordingly.

13

Your Professional Advisers: Putting It All Together

Planning your estate, as we have discussed in the preceding chapters, requires detailed knowledge and experience in a variety of disciplines. To realize your goals, you should not undertake estate-planning by yourself. Meeting your objectives will require time and some effort on your part, and also the cooperation of your spouse and perhaps other family members. In addition, you will need certain professionals who specialize in several different but allied fields to guide you along the correct legal and financial path. All are important pieces in the estate-planning puzzle. Your concern and direction in the process will dictate when and to what extent the professionals are needed, but they should always be available to you for consultation and discussion. Your team of advisers are listed here and their functions described in more detail in the sections following.

Estate-Planning Attorney
Executor (Personal Representative)
Bank and Trust Companies
Stock Brokerage Firm
Independent Money Manager
Financial Planner, Investment Adviser, Investment Counsel

Insurance Agent
Accountant

Estate-Planning Attorney

You may think it is simple to find a lawyer who fits your personal and estate planning needs, but it may not be that easy. Those with the good reputations always appear to be too busy and seem to charge the most. A good candidate for an estate-planning attorney would be one with a high level of competence, a concern for you and your family's interests, and one whom you can trust. He or she should currently be practicing in the field of estates, trusts, and wills and have a minimum of ten years experience in drafting these instruments, with a current emphasis grounded in tax law. A master's degree in taxation wouldn't hurt. You should *not* hire an attorney who says he or she knows estate planning but whose background doesn't validate this claim. No one can be an expert in everything. Just about any lawyer can draft a will or a simple trust agreement. You need a competent attorney to reduce the risk of error in the agreement or a flaw anywhere in the process, which could remain undetected until after your death and be costly for your estate.

Having the right person is especially important if you need to create a more complicated trust agreement—perhaps a grantor-retained annuity trust, a charitable lead trust, or a trust protecting the special needs of a minor child. None can be drafted by someone familiar with only the boiler plate variety of trust agreement taken from a computer software program. The attorney you hire needs, in addition, to be familiar with the workings of the probate court so it doesn't take more time than necessary to have your estate settled. And an even more important asset is his or her empathetic approach to your particular situation. You will be sharing information of a highly personal nature, and therefore you must have confidence and trust in this person.

Although association memberships do not carry much weight nor indicate to you how effective your prospective candidate will be, such memberships may tell you to what extent this person is involved and committed in his or her chosen field. Being a member of an active association can acquaint the attorney with pending new legislation and changes in the tax laws. Some of the associations are the American College of Trust and Estate Council, your local estate planning council, the tax section and the estates and trusts section of your local bar association, and the National Academy of Elder Law Attorneys.

Bar association referral services should be suspect, and generally the screening as to specialization and other legal skills is perfunctory at best. It may be worthwhile checking with them, however, if you have no one else. The more traditional approach to finding a lawyer is the personal route, that is, a recommendation from someone whom you respect or from an organization that you are familiar with and in which the prospective candidate had performed well.

Once you have chosen the attorney with whom you feel comfortable, it would be wise to have at least one consultation regarding your estate and have recommendations made to you as to how to best reflect your intentions in a legal document. In all probability, other advisers would be brought into the picture to design a plan that would attempt to achieve the goals that you have set out to accomplish for yourself and your beneficiaries. This team would also be available later on, to your executor who will have the responsibility of coordinating the postmortem administration and final disposition of your estate as it was planned.

Estate-Planning Worksheet

Once you have made some decisions as to how you would like your estate apportioned, to which charities you might like to leave some money, who would receive the summer home, or what schooling to provide for a distant cousin, it would be wise to provide as much pertinent financial information to your attorney and other members of your team of professionals. A statement of your net worth, in addition to other information that is compiled on an estate-planning worksheet, shown in Figure 13.1, will be a great aid to those professionals offering suggestions on how to proceed with the plan.

The worksheet, properly filled in, clearly shows what you own and what you owe. Assets are listed and categorized by the type and form of ownership and should indicate on a separate sheet your original cost basis of the asset, in addition to its present value. It would ordinarily include among other things, total current income, including pension and retirement income and any inheritances that may be forthcoming. In addition, current liabilities and projections of future liabilities need to be considered. Figure 13.1 gives an example of one type of estate-planning worksheet (in a reduced size format). Employing a worksheet will not only be helpful to you but is an absolute necessity for your attorney and other professionals who will need this information to help plan your estate properly. In addition to financial information, your attorney needs to know addresses and telephone numbers of close family and friends, your official domicile, that is, where your estate will be probated, what, if any, real or personal property you currently own in other jurisdictions, locations of safe-deposit box(es) and the keys and contents, such as marital agreements, insurance policies, income tax returns, deeds, contracts, buy-sell agreements, death and marriage certificates, any records of earlier marriages and any former spouse or children from a previous marriage able to place a claim against your estate.

If you are making a new will, then a statement that all prior wills are to be revoked is a necessity, and you must notify any lawyer you previously used. Any charitable bequests should be mentioned. Last, and perhaps most important, a statement of your goals or objectives must be written out, describing what you want to accomplish monetarily in providing for certain family members or other beneficiaries by gift or legacy. It should be specific. Describe the amount of the bequest and to whom it is to be made. A specific legacy is one that reads, "I give and bequeath or devise to my dear friend, John J. Jones, my entire coin collection." It takes precedence over a more general legacy that comes out of the general assets of the estate.

The Executor

In whatever manner you have chosen to dispose of your property, you will require a person or entity to be responsible for the supervision and transfer of your estate after you die. If you have a will, you need to appoint an executor (personal representative) to take over. Similarly, a living revocable trust in which you have acted as trustee and that continues after your death must name a successor trustee to see that your wishes and instructions are carried out. This person, or perhaps financial institution, accepts the responsibility for the investment management and general administration of the trust and is considered to be a fiduciary, who assumes the legal duty to act in a dependable manner for the benefit of your family and others named.

The executor's duties, as discussed in a previous chap-

ESTATE-PLANNING WORKSHEET FORMAT

ASSETS	Current Values	Name on Title	Yearly Income
Savings:			
C.D.s:			
Checking;			
Money Market:			
Life Insurance (Cash Value)			
Business Interests:			
Collectibles			
Personal Property			
Equity in Home: (Cost: Date Purchased:)			
Retirement Income: Annuities, pensions			
Household Property:			
Automobile(s):			
Securities: (Stocks, Bonds, and Mutual Funds), etc.			
Accounts Receivable:			
Promissory Note Receivable:			
Investment Property (Cost: Date Purchased:)			
Miscellaneous:			
TOTAL ASSETS:			
Liabilities	Current Values	Name on Title	Yearly Expenses
Accounts Payable: (Credit Cards, etc.):			
Loans on Personal Property: (Auto, Furniture):			
Other Loans:			
Mortgage on Residence:			
Other mortgages on Real Estate:			
TOTAL LIABILITIES			
Other Facts			
1. Anticipated Death Benefits Life Insurance:			
2. Anticipated gifts or inheritance from others (Amount if possible)			

Figure 13.1

ter, are mainly to protect the property of the decedent from loss or harm and, among other things, make the decedent's legal claim(s) against third parties, pay expenses and debts attributable to the decedent, prepare and file tax returns with the help of the accountant, value inventory, collect assets, and liquidate certain assets when necessary. The executor's job can be lengthy, time consuming, and last two to three years. Whoever accepts it is legally responsible for the decisions made and any reckless or imprudent behavior on the part of the executor can make that person(s) or entity legally liable for any financial losses of estate income.

After speaking with your attorney on possible candidates for executor of your estate, and after you have prepared your will, you should complete a *letter of instructions* and give it to your executor and at least two members of your family. The letter should describe the location of records pertinent to your estate and the addresses and phone numbers of family members and those of advisers from whom you have sought professional help. It would be similar to the sample letter of instruction in Figure 13.2.

Bank and Trust Companies

Most major banks maintain trust departments that furnish customers with a variety of services, including trust management. Private trust companies also provide a similar purpose. Both supply many of the following services:

- Serve as custodian, trustee, or successor trustee
- Review assets in the portfolio on a quarterly basis
- Make recommendations and give a choice of investment objectives, including determining the percent-

Burial Instructions
    Name of the Religious Institution:
    Location:
    Phone No.:
    Name of Minister, Priest, Rabbi:
    Location of Religious Institution, Phone No.:
    Names and addresses of Significant Family Members:
    Names and addresses of Beneficiaries:

Advisers

	Name	*Address*	*Phone*
Executor			
Stockbroker:			
Attorney:			
Insurance Agent:			
Accountant:			
Bank Officer:			
Real Estate Agent:			

Records   *Location*

    Ownership of Burial Plot
    Will, Trust Document
    Stock Certificates
    Certificates of Deposits
    Mortgage(s)
    Promissory Notes
    Deed(s)
    Checkbook, Bank Statements
    Income tax returns
    Marriage certificate
    Birth certificate
    Social Security card
    Insurance policies (Life, Home, etc.)
    Safe-Deposit Box(es)

Figure 13.2   Information Conveyed in Letter of Instruction

age of your money that should be allocated to different types of securities within your portfolio
- Recommend when sales should take place to obtain cash when necessary
- Send periodic statements on investment perform- ance
- Give analyses of your portfolio's rate of return
- Consult on meeting current needs and those of your beneficiaries in the future
- Help you with tax planning
- Appraise, collect, and deliver assets to any particu- lar location
- Collect dividends and interest if necessary
- Value securities at death

Of course, what the bank or trust company will do de- pends on how much you are paying them and what ser- vices they have agreed to perform. They generally charge for everything, including acceptance and termination fees and reimbursement fees for out-of-pocket expenses. Your attorney will work with the trust officer because he or she has experience in the everyday operation of es- tates. If any administrative problems arise, especially in postmortem management, the trust officer should be able to find the proper answers and solutions.

Because banks and trust companies are fiduciaries, most of them tend to be more conservative in their in- vestment philosophy and approach to investing than an investment management or advisory firm. Because the reputations of private (nonbank and nontrust) managers are based on their success in beating the stock market averages, there is some tendency on their part to suggest that higher risk securities be placed in portfolios. Banks and trust companies are more interested in preserving assets in the estate and therefore, in general, have a tendency to focus on safer, less risky investments and are willing to accept a smaller long-term total rate of return.

Stock Brokerage Firms

Stock brokerage firms, in the past, have offered a limited amount of financial choices to their clients, mostly concentrating in the area of stocks and bonds. Now, however, these large financial organizations have become investment bankers selling shares of stock to clients in large public offerings, marketing various types of insurance and annuity products, doing option trading, buying and selling municipal bonds, mutual funds, and all types of government securities. They also provide investment management services and can buy and sell foreign currencies; some even have their own trust companies.

Most large full service firms are members of the New York Stock Exchange, but this membership does not insure that you will receive better service. Your account might be safer, however, because larger firms tend to have more stringent capital requirements and generally carry additional private insurance on each account. The brokerage firm is represented by individual sales representatives, sometimes called brokers, account executives, or investment counselors. They are fairly well trained, work on a commission basis, and also give advice, although one must question how good it is?

Discount brokers, on the other hand, generally give no advice but merely execute your buy or sell orders. Usually they have smaller offices, employ fewer people, and consequently can charge much less than a full-service brokerage firm, running what can be described as a no-frills operation. My personal experience with them has been positive. I have found them to be prompt and courteous, on time with delivery of confirmations, generally crediting current interest on cash balances comparable to what other firms give, and overall functioning as brokerage firms. If you want more service than that, you will have to pay for it through a much (two to three times) higher commission schedule at one of the large brokerage firms. Using a discounter depends on the kind of service you need. If your account is very prominent in your estate planning and you are not enthusiastic about doing research, or do not have the flair, inclination, background, or temperament to do your own investing, and do value advice (whether good or bad), then you should stay with a full-service brokerage firm. If, on the other hand, you wish to make your own decisions and you do not need someone to talk with everyday, go with a good discount broker. They execute, buy, and sell orders for you or your trust that are error free, and they provide a basic level of assistance for you if there are any problems.

Independent Money Managers and Other Financial Advisers

The people who can offer you financial advice come in many different forms, and it is not always easy to distinguish which is best for you. Many provide the same services with slightly different emphasis. Let's start off with the money managers.

The *independent money manager* can be an individual or a company, not necessarily affiliated with any financial institution, that manages the portfolios of others on a fee-based schedule. Fees are assessed on the total market value of securities under management. Through an agreement, you as owner give the manager control over the selection of securities in your personal account or perhaps in an account in which you exercise authority, such as a revocable trust.

To start an account with a money manager, you generally need to have an existing account or open a new one at a stock brokerage firm. A trading authorization is signed by you to permit the money manager to give buy and sell orders to your brokerage firm account executive. The stock brokerage firm will send confirmations of current transactions, in addition to a monthly activity statement of transactions that have taken place in the preceding period. Most of the paper work comes to you directly from the brokerage house because the account is titled in your name or in the name of a trust.

Independent money managers must be very effective in order for them to be worth the fee that you pay them. This fee will reduce your overall rate of return from investments, and you still have to pay sales commissions to the broker. The advantage in hiring a manager, however, is that you receive individualized attention for your investments, and there is usually complete objectivity involved in the decision-making process. The manager has nothing to sell other than the service performed and receives no commissions. In choosing a manager, you must do research in the same way you do when selecting an estate-planning lawyer or a trust company. It can be a lengthy process, and therefore should be done when you have the time to spend on it.

Investment advisers are somewhat like independent money managers but they are usually broader based in their knowledge and handle more than just investment securities. The Securities and Exchange Commission (SEC) requires registration of people who receive compensation for giving investment advice. *Registered Investment Advisers* (RIAs) pay a registration fee with the SEC and provide information on their work background and education but are not specifically required to offer standardized or formal degree requirements or other university credentials prior to the title being used. This is also true of other managers and financial advisers previously mentioned in this chapter. An RIA will review your assets and give you advice on improving your long-term rate of return in addition to managing your portfolio of securities.

A person with numerous investments and a complex set of personal and business arrangements may want to hire a *financial planning firm* to create a comprehensive financial plan stating goals and receiving opinions, or to give advice on a limited basis on a plan already in place. If you fall into either of these categories the planning firm can gather professionals that it works with, representing different disciplines, and provide you with assistance in establishing a financial plan. Initially you will be asked to complete a financial data worksheet similar to Figure 13.1. The firm, after consulting with you, will then prepare a report offering you suggestions on budgeting, do a cost of living analysis, and provide you with strategies that you might follow on investments, retirement planning, insurance and annuities, and other financial assets. Anything more complicated, such as tax and estate planning, that use the creative devices found in this book would probably require more in-depth conferences with specialists in their respective fields.

Financial planners are generally people who have been trained as stock brokers, insurance agents, accountants or bank officers. Some are very well trained and others, perhaps not. Passing a certification test that covers many areas of investments is required to become a *certified financial planner* (CFP). CFPs seek compensation in different ways: (1) fee-only planners who charge by the hour and bill you after creating and submitting a formalized plan to you, (2) commission *and* fee firms that receive commissions from the company (such as insurance companies) or a stock brokerage firm and may also but not generally charge for their time, and (3) commission-only planners who do not charge a planning fee, but receive compensation from the company whose product they sell.

How much you are able to do yourself and your level of competency in the financial area will determine whether paying an initial and probably additional layer of expenses is worthwhile. After all, you are still going to pay either directly or indirectly your estate-planning attorney, accountant, and any stock brokerage transactional fees or mutual fund loads that are part of your plan. If you do feel you need help and decide to go the CFP route, consider very carefully the firm you hire and compare it with other options in the money management area that are available to advise you. Regardless of how astute and proficient the planner may be, *you*, or the one *you appoint* to handle your affairs, will still have to make important policy decisions.

Finding and hiring the "right" planner can also take time. For some initial information, you might telephone the National Association of Personal Financial Planners (800) 366-2732 or The Institute of Certified Financial Planners (800) 282-7526. They should be able to direct you to several planning firms in your geographical area. Trying one or two on a trial basis before signing any agreement for the development of a plan might also be wise.

The *investment counsel*, also, is a firm or individual who provides investment services and research for you. Its attention to your needs is completely objective because it sells nothing but a service. Generally, the counsel may have an affiliation with a stock brokerage firm, but its independence should not be questioned. The counsel makes investment recommendations to you or a trustee and if acceptable the order to buy or sell securities is acted upon. Your degree of involvement in investment decisions will be determined by prior agreement.

Some counseling firms do not accept small accounts, but usually require a $100,000 minimum in assets, with a fee schedule based on a percentage of the total value of the managed portfolio. The percentage charged generally decreases as the account value increases.

Life Insurance Agent

Buying life insurance today is a much more complex operation than it was in the past. Insurance companies now offer a plethora of options and alternatives that require more expertise on the part of the one purchasing the policy. The insurance agent must advise you on what insurance products are most appropriate for you and your family. A well-trained, honest, and experienced insurance representative should discuss with you how a particular policy will help you with your estate planning. A variety of planning options can include the use of trusts, annual gifting, probate avoidance, and the idea of leveraging your death benefit, tax savings, and financial security for your surviving spouse and beneficiaries. The agent, with the help of your attorney, should attempt to coordinate smoothly an insurance program with an existing estate plan.

The Accountant

The accountant works closely with your lawyer in preparing all tax returns that must be filed—income tax, fiduciary, and, later on, estate tax returns. Records of all prior year's returns and reports must be maintained. Property values have great significance in determining how much your estate will pay in taxes. If the estate is overvalued, then the tax will be increased proportionately. If it is undervalued, your tax will be less, but the IRS may attempt to contest the valuation, which may lead to litigation expenses. The accountant can handle any tax problem with the Internal Revenue Service. In addition, an accountant can make analyses of your financial condition, keep a close watch on any changes in the tax code, and alert you and your lawyer as to its effects on your estate-planning program. If property is involved, the accountant is usually aware of the changing values, especially when there are probatable assets whose value have not been determined. The accountant also confers with the appraiser and the executor of the estate to do an inventory analysis and a valuation procedure regarding the estate's worth.

When a corporate trustee is not involved, the accountant generally is made responsible for tax filings. However, if a trust does prepare statements and tax returns, the accountant should receive copies of the statements to validate their correctness and tell you or, after your death, inform the executor, if there are any problems. If you have had the same accountant for many years, he or she pretty much knows most of the required information and has access to all of your prior tax returns. A new accountant, however, would require copies of at least three years of federal and state tax returns and all pertinent and important information, such as the cost basis for appreciated assets, confirmations of securities transactions, and records of capital improvements on your home.

Coordinating Your Estate Plan

After you have consulted with all your advisers, and feel you have a good idea of what you would like to accomplish, your attorney is the one you have to see if you and he or she haven't already had preliminary discussions. Be prepared to state your objectives and try to be as precise as possible as to how you think you would like to proceed. Your attorney will reflect on what you say and offer suggestions as to what you might do. You will have a better understanding of what is said because you now have the background to consider not only suggestions that are made, but also whether or not you and your attorney are on the same track. Each of you has to be clear in what is said, know the meaning of any possible action taken, and evaluate the long-term effect on any decision.

One thing to always be on the lookout for is miscommunication between you and your advisers. If there is a strategy you wish to advance, or one that is suggested to you as part of the plan, don't let it pass with a weak "yes" if you really don't think you understand fully the broad implications involved. Becoming synchronized with your adviser's thinking is vitally important for the success of your plan. For instance, in the area of money management and the selection of an investment portfolio, you and the one managing your money must be certain that you both understand the level of risk that you are and are not willing to accept. If the discussion centers around the establishment of a trust, you and your attorney should be in agreement as to how much money should be placed into the trust. An appropriate amount would be consistent with what you and your spouse's current needs are, and what your future requirements might be, based on the quality of life you both would like to pursue. Placing too much money in a trust might jeopardize those requirements.

When you and your attorney have agreed on an overall estate plan, a discussion of costs involving the preparation and later execution of documents would be appropriate. If the fees seem to be fair, you should have your attorney prepare the documents and study them very carefully and decide whether or not they reflect your exact intentions as to what you wish to accomplish. If they do not, then do not hesitate to make changes at that time without putting it off to some later date.

Reviewing and Updating Your Documents

Every so often you should have all your agreements, papers, records, and all legal documents reviewed by your estate-planning team. Federal, state, and local laws change, circumstances may be different, and what you have done may not be appropriate currently. This is especially true when your family situation has in some way been modified and a possible update is required if your plan is to stay effective. It should be reviewed especially when

1. There is a dramatic change in your health or the health of your spouse;
2. The death of a spouse or another significant member of your family occurs.
3. A new marriage or the dissolution of one takes place.
4. A substantial increase or decrease in the size of your estate, perhaps an inheritance, occurs.
5. There appears to be a significant attitude change in a beneficiary.
6. There is a modification in the tax law, trust law, probate law, or property law.
7. A medical problem occurs causing a change in your insurability if you are acquiring insurance.
8. You or your spouse purchase property in another state.
9. The birth of a child or grandchild occurs.
10. You change your domicile.

11. You retire from a business or profession.
12. The death, or the inability to perform, of a successor trustee, personal representative, or guardian takes place.

Some Final Thoughts

We have discussed the professionals and advisers that are necessary to you in developing an effective estate plan. Although they are your team, the most important member of the team is you. Little will be accomplished unless you make it happen. Your plan will not take shape unless you pick up the planning reins and take the first and second steps. You are the one who must recognize the importance of arranging your assets in such a way that they will benefit not only yourself, but your spouse, family, and other possible beneficiaries. You are a generalist coordinating your team of professionals in attempting to design and arrange a workable estate plan for your family's future. You should be well organized, methodical, and willing to accept goal-oriented planning techniques involving the variety of disciplines discussed in this book that will increase the value of your assets during the rest of your life and also provide for the tax-free transfer of as much property as possible to spouse, family, and others, under current law. Cutting through a sometimes confusing maze of information will be a challenge, but the basic foundation of knowledge can be absorbed by you with some timely guidance and direction coming from your professional team gathered to help.

What I have tried to do in this book is to touch on certain basic concepts and offer ideas and suggestions for planning the proper maintenance, transfer, distribution, and disposition of your estate to family members and others. If this is done with great care, your family should receive the most benefit from what you have worked for. In designing your estate plan, try not to make it too rigid. All of us experience change in our personal lives, including our economic situation. This is a fact of life. Parents die, children are born and quickly grow up. Families increase in size. College expenses must be paid. Children marry, grandchildren are born, retirement comes, and the cycle continues unabated. So flexibility should be in your mind as you create your plan and make modifications as circumstances change.

If you have done your homework, it will be a good estate plan. Indeed, it can be a vital factor in leaving as much of your hard-earned assets to your heirs and beneficiaries. Doing this properly will take some time and effort on your part. Your plan should not be to save every tax dollar possible, but to decide on the wisest plan for the disposition of your assets to those persons whom *you* choose. Good luck.

Appendix I

For Further Information

Advocates For Older People
2136 Pennsylvania Ave., NW
Washington, DC 20052
(202) 676-5133

American Association of Retired Persons [AARP]
601 E St., NW
Washington, DC 20049
(202) 434-277

American Bar Assocation
Commission on Legal Problems For the Elderly
740 Fifteenth St., NW
Washington, DC 20005
(202) 662-1000

American College of Trust & Estate Counsel
3415 Sepulveda Blvd., Suite 460
Los Angeles, CA 90034
(310) 572-7280

American Council of Life Insurance
1001 Pennsylvania Ave., NW, Suite 500
Washington, DC 20004
(202) 624-2000

Association of Private Pension and Welfare Plans
1212 New York Ave., NW
Washington, DC 20005
(202) 289-6700

Federal Deposit Insurance Corporation
550 Seventeenth Street, NW
Washington, DC 20429
(202) 393-8400

Federal Reserve Board
Twentieth & C Streets, NW
Washington, DC 20551
(202) 452-3000

HALT (An organization of Americans for legal reform)
1319 F St., Suite 300
Washington, DC 20004
(202) 347-9600

Institute of Certified Financial Planners
3443 South Galena, Suite 190
Denver, CO 80231-5093
(303) 751-7600

Internal Revenue Service
(800) 829-1040
(800) 829-3676
Forms: 706: U.S. Estate Tax Return
709: U.S. Gift Tax Return
709A: U.S. Short Form Gift Tax Return

Publications #s
#448: Federal Estate and Gift Taxes
#526: Charitable Contributions
#554: Tax Information for Older Americans
#590: IRAs
#915: Social Security Benefits

#559: Tax Information for Survivors,
Executors, and Administrators
#564: Mutual Fund Distributions
#560: Self-Employed Retirement Plans

Legal Counsel For the Elderly
601 E St., NW
Building A, 4th Floor
Washington, DC 20004
(202) 234-0970

National Academy of Elder Law Attorneys
655 N. Alveron Way, Suite 108
Tucson, AZ 85711
(602) 881-4005

National Council of Senior Citizens
925 Fifteenth St.
Washington, DC 20005
(202) 347-8800

National Association of Securities Dealers, Inc.
1735 K St., NW
Washington, DC 20006
(202) 728-8000

National Council on the Aging
West Wing 100
600 Maryland Ave., SW
Washington, DC 20024
(202) 479-1200

National Senior Citizens Law Center
1815 H St. NW, Suite 700
Washington, DC 20006
(202) 887-5280

New York Stock Exchange
11 Wall St.
New York, NY 10005
(212) 656-3000

Pension Benefit Guaranty Corporation
1200 K St. NW
Washington, DC 20006
(202) 326-4000

Securities and Exchange Commission
450 Fifth St. NW
Washington, DC 20549
(202) 272-7440

Glossary

A-B Trust: A way to provide for your surviving spouse and protect the interests of your children or other beneficiaries.

Accrued interest: The interest earned on an investment since the last interest payment.

Acknowledgment: A statement made in front of a notary public that a document with your signature was actually signed by you.

Actuary: A person professionally trained in the technical and mathematical aspects of life insurance.

Adjusted gross income: The gross income less legitimate business expenses and losses.

Administrator: The person named by the court to represent the estate when there is no will or the will did not name an executor.

Advance Medical Directive: A legal instrument that allows you to effectively communicate your precise medical choices and preferences when treatment or medical decisions are required.

Affidavit: A statement that is notarized and signed under oath by anyone having personal knowledge of the facts; these statements are used to support facts contained in documents submitted to the court.

Annual exclusion: The amount you can gift each year per donee without having to file a return or pay gift taxes; $10,000 is the limit for individuals, $20,000 for a married couple making a gift jointly.

Annuity: Payments made to you or a named beneficiary for a specific period or at regular intervals by an insurance company with whom an annuity contract exists.

Annuity trust: A type of trust that will pay you a set amount each year while you are alive.

Appraiser: An expert who determines the market or fair value of an asset.

Asset: A word used to describe anything that you own, including real estate, life insurance, royalties, jewelry, art, furniture, clothing, automobiles, stocks, bonds, mutual funds, bank accounts, certificates of deposit (CDs), government securities, gold, silver, and collectibles.

Attestation clause: A statement at the end of the will saying that the witnesses saw the testator sign, in their presence, and that they then signed in his or her presence and in each other's presence.

Attorney-in-fact: Under a power of attorney, the person named to act as legal agent for the person who gives the power of attorney.

Average cost—single category: An accounting method to determine your average cost basis for mutual fund ownership and the reporting of capital gains.

Beneficial interest: The right to enjoy or profit from property held in trust; the person with the beneficial interest is the beneficiary.

Beneficiary: A person who is entitled to receive benefits (usually money or other property) from a trust or an estate.

Bequest: A gift of property at death; technically, inherited real estate is called a "devise" while all other types of assets are called "bequests."

Bond: A debt instrument of a private or public corporation or a state or federal government that promises to pay a specified amount of money on a certain day in the future.

Bypass trust: A trust that is set up to bypass the surviving spouse's estate, thereby allowing full use of the $600,000 federal estate tax exemption for both spouses. The trust typically created by a married couple to contain property that will not be included, for estate tax purposes, in the estate of the surviving spouse. The surviving spouse receives income from the trust but not the principal. A name sometimes used to describe the B part of an A-B Trust.

Charitable lead trust: A trust that donates to a charity the income from trust assets while reserving the assets themselves for later distribution to other beneficiaries.

Charitable remainder trust: A trust that pays income from trust assets to the donor or beneficiaries while reserving the assets for later contribution to the charity.

Class: One or more beneficiaries, or their heirs, that is described only by status; common examples are "children," "grandchildren," and "issue."

Codicil: A written change or amendment to a will.

Common property: The property that is held by two or more parties under one of the forms of co-ownership, i.e., joint tenancy, tenancy in common, tenancy by the entirety, or community property.

Common stock: A security that represents ownership of assets of a corporation.

Community property: In community property states the property held jointly by husband and wife and acquired during their marriage by the efforts of either or both of them.

Conservator: An individual appointed by the court to administrate the affairs of an incapacitated adult.

Contingent beneficiary: A person or organization that is entitled to part or all of an estate left by will or trust if the original beneficiaries are unable to accept.

Contingent interest: The interest in property that is dependent not on the passage of time but on the occurrence of a future event, such as a college graduation.

Convenience account: An account—usually a bank account—that has been opened in joint names but for the convenience of only one of the joint owners and not with the intent that the noncontributing owner receive the balance in the account. As a result, the account could be part of a deceased owner's probate estate.

Corporate trustee: A bank, trust company, or large brokerage firm, which specializes in managing trusts and/or is listed as a trustee in the trust document.

Corpus: Latin word for "body"; the main part of a thing (like a trust or will): for example, the principal placed in a trust.

Cost basis: What you paid for the personal property or real estate.

Cotenant: One of the owners under a cotenancy.

Cotrustee: Another person, often a family member, who serves with the trustee in helping to make decisions concerning the trust.

Creator: The person who creates a trust by providing money or property for it; see also donor, grantor, settlor, trustor.

Credit estate tax: The state tax on the assets of someone who has died. It applies only in some states and only to estates that are required to pay federal estate taxes.

Credit shelter trust: Another name for bypass trust or A-B trust.

Creditor: A person or entity that is owed money or property.

Crummey letter: A written notification to beneficiaries that a gift has been made to an irrevocable life-insurance trust.

Custodian: A person or entity named to manage the financial affairs of a minor; only the custodian has the power to buy, sell, or transfer assets in the minor's account.

Death tax: Another name for inheritance and estate taxes.

Decedent: The person who has died.

Devise: A gift of real estate under a will.

Disclaimer: When a beneficiary or heir under a will, or a trust, does not wish to accept the bequest, he or she may disclaim it without tax consequences if he or she does so within a certain time established by law.

Diversification: Spreading the risk by investing in many different companies and industries.

Dollar-cost averaging: Investing equal amounts of money at regular intervals.

Domicile: The place where a person permanently resides, even though he or she may not spend all or even a majority of his or her time there.

Donee: A person who receives a gift.

Donor: A person who makes a gift.

Durable power of attorney: The legal document whereby one person authorizes another to make medical *and* financial decisions should illness or incapacitation occur.

Durable power of attorney for health care: The legal document whereby one person authorizes another to make health-care decisions should illness or incapacitation occur; this power terminates upon revocation or death of its maker.

Estate tax: A transfer tax imposed on the value of property left at death; often called a death tax.

Executor: The person or institution named in a will who is responsible for the management of the assets and the ultimate transfer of the property; also referred to as a personal representative.

Expenses of administration: The costs incurred by the estate's executor or administrator in carrying out the terms of your will or intestate succession.

Family limited partnership: A way to use a partnership arrangement to shift assets to other family members with reduced tax consequences.

Family trust: In common usage, a trust agreement that provides for a certain portion of the estate or trust to be set aside in a separate trust to operate for the benefit of the family (spouse or children or both).

Federal estate tax: The federal tax assessed against the assets of a person who has died if the value of the taxable assets exceeds $600,000.

Fiduciary: Person in a position of trust and confidence; a person who has a duty to act primarily for the benefit of another. A trustee or executor acts as a fiduciary.

Future interest: A right to property that can be enforced sometime in the future.

Generation-skipping tax: A large tax on assets that skip a generation and are left instead to grandchildren or great-grandchildren rather than to one's children.

Generation-skipping trust: A type of trust that is structured so that the children are given either nothing or only income for life, with the actual principal passing to the grandchildren or great-grand-children.

Gift: The transfer of property from one individual to another without consideration (payment).

Gift tax: A tax imposed on transfers of property by gift during the donor's lifetime.

Gift tax exclusion: The law permits the exclusion each year of the first $10,000 in gifts made to any one donee; married couples may jointly gift tax free up to $20,000 to any number of donees.

Grantor: Also known as a trustor or settlor, this is the person who creates the trust.

Grantor retained income trust (GRIT): An irrevocable trust into which the grantor places property and retains the income and the use of the property for a number of years.

Gross estate: The value of an estate before debts are paid, mortgages subtracted, and funeral costs taken out; this is also the value used to determine probate fees.

Growth fund: A mutual fund whose primary investment objective is capital appreciation.

Guardian: One who is legally responsible for the care and well being of a minor. Appointed by a court, the guardian is under court supervision.

Heir: The person or persons who will inherit according to the laws of a state when a person dies without a will.

Holographic will: A will that is completely handwritten by the testator and signed and dated by him, with or without witnesses. An unwitnessed holographic will is valid in only a few states.

Incidents of ownership: Control over a life-insurance policy; this usually means that the policy will be included as part of the decedent's estate if he or she possesses any hint of ownership.

Income: All financial gains from investments, work, or business.

Income beneficiary: A beneficiary of a trust who receives only the income generated by the trust assets.

Income fund: A mutual fund whose primary objective is income.

Incompetent: A person who has been legally declared by a court to be unable to handle his own affairs.

Inheritance tax: The tax imposed on property received by beneficiaries from the estate of a decedent.

Insurance trust: A trust that owns and manages a life insurance policy and designates its beneficiaries.

Intangible personal property: Property other than real estate and other than property that can be "touched." Stocks are intangible property.

Inter-vivos trust: A trust that takes effect during the lifetime of its maker. A living trust is a type of inter-vivos trust.

Intestate: When used as an adjective, it means to be without a valid will; as a noun, one who has no valid will.

Intestate succession: The rules established by your estate to determine who receives property after your death if a valid will and/or trust does not exist.

Inventory: A listing of assets and their respective values that will be needed if your estate is subject to probate.

Irrevocable trust: Similar to a revocable trust except in that once signed, an irrevocable trust cannot be revoked or changed in any way.

Issue: One's offspring or descendants. Your children, grandchildren, great-grandchildren, and so forth, are your issue.

Joint tenancy with rights of survivorship: A form of ownership in which property is equally shared by all owners and is automatically transferred to the surviving owners when one of them dies.

Laws of intestacy: The laws of a state that dictate to whom the intestacy property of a person dying intestate will be distributed.

Legacy: A gift of personal property made in a will. Basically, the same thing as a bequest.

Letters testamentary: Papers issued by the probate court, that authorize the executor to probate the estate of the deceased.

Life estate: A gift or inheritance in which the donee is able to use the property during his or her lifetime.

Life-insurance trust: An irrevocable trust designed so that your life-insurance premiums are paid by the trust so that the death benefit is not included as part of your estate.

Liquidity: That which is easily and quickly converted to cash with substantial price concession.

Living trust: A document that creates a legally recognized entity; (a trust) into which you place some or all of your assets and have someone or some entity manage it for the benefit of you, your spouse, children, and others.

Living will: A document stating that you do not want to be kept alive by artificial means if the injury, illness, or condition is terminal; it is not actually a will but a directive.

Load: An acquisition fee paid initially to purchase shares of a load mutual fund.

Marital deduction: A deduction that is available for transfers between spouses, either during lifetime or at death; under federal law, there is a complete interspousal exemption from transfer tax for qualifying transfers.

Marketability: The measure of the ease with which a security can be sold.

Minor: A person considered by law to be under the age of discretion. It can be eighteen or twenty-one, depending on the jurisdiction.

Mutual Will: Two separate wills with substantially identical provisions.

Net estate tax due: The taxes due on an estate after credits and deductions have been subtracted.

Net value: What estate-tax liability is based on. The value of an estate after all debts, mortgages, burial costs, and other final expenses have been deducted.

Odd-Lot: A block of stock consisting of fewer shares than the number customarily traded at one time (a round lot of 100 shares).

Personal property: Everything that is not real estate (real property), including cash, securities, bank accounts, jewelry, art, collections, etc.

Personal representative: Another name for the executor or administrator of an estate.

Petition: A document filed with the court requesting certain action.

Pooled-income fund: A charitable remainder trust managed by a charity in which contributions from several donors are combined and managed jointly.

Pour-over Will: A will that is used in conjunction with a revocable living trust to pour over any assets that are not transferred to the trust prior to death.

Power of appointment: Giving someone the power to dispose of someone else's property.

Power of attorney: A written statement by which a person (the "principal") authorizes another person (Attorney-in-fact) to act for him or her in a limited or general capacity.

Preferred stock: A security that receives preference over common stock with respect to dividends and claims against assets.

Present interest: The right to use property immediately, as opposed to a future interest.

Probate: A process that validates a will (if there is one). An executor or administrator is appointed, debts and taxes are paid, heirs are identified, and property distributed.

Prospectus: A booklet describing a mutual fund or any enterprise and offering its shares for sale.

Qualified terminable interest property ("Q-Tip") trust: A terminable interest that will qualify for the marital deduction, if an appropriate election is made by the donor or executor. This type of vehicle is frequently used to avoid any transfer tax upon the death of the first spouse; it provides the surviving spouse with all the income from the property during his or her life, but it enables the deceased spouse to retain control over the ultimate disposition of the property.

Real property: Real estate, land, permanent fixtures (kitchen cabinets, bath fixtures, etc.), and mineral rights.

Remainder interest: An interest in property that follows an estate for years or for life.

Remainderman: The person who receives part or all of a trust's assets once the trust is terminated; usually there is nothing left.

Residence: The physical location a person considers to be his or her home; normally, a person can have only one residence for purposes of estate settlement.

Residuary estate: Whatever remains of the estate after payment of debts, expenses, taxes, and specific bequests. In a pour-over will, the residuary estate is left to a living trust.

Reversionary interest: The assets that pass on to another person because a condition was either fulfilled or not met.

Revocable trust: A trust plan that gives the grantor the power to alter the trust terms or revoke the trust.

Rights of survivorship: The right of a joint tenant (but not a tenant-in-common) to take the whole of the jointly held property if he survives the other joint tenant(s).

Rule against perpetuities: A law that requires all trusts to terminate by the time everyone mentioned in the trust dies plus twenty-one years.

Self-proving will: A will that allows the court to accept it as valid without further proof; a will that was properly witnessed.

Settlor: A person who establishes a trust. Another name for grantor.

Spendthrift clause: Provision included in some trusts that prohibits the beneficiary from giving or selling to others the beneficiary's rights to the trust's assets or income.

Sprinkling trust: A trust under which the trustee has discretion to make distributions among two or more beneficiaries in accordance with certain guidelines.

Standby trust: A living trust that takes effect if a grantor becomes ill or incapacitated or dies. The grantor's assets are transferred to the trust and managed by the designated trustee.

State estate tax: A tax levied in states that wish to utilize the state death tax credit permitted by the federal estate tax return.

Stepped-up cost basis: A (usually) increased tax cost that takes effect when property is received as the result of a person's death.

Successor executor: A person named in a will to replace the first-named executor if for any reason he or she is not able to serve.

Successor trustee: Person who takes over the rights and responsibilities of an original trustee.

Surety Bond: A bond, that is unless waived, required for an executor or administrator before he or she can be actively involved with the estate.

Tangible personal property: Property other than real estate that has inherent value and can be touched, such as jewelry, furniture, clothing, automobiles, boats, machinery, etc.

Tenancy by the entirety: A special form of joint tenancy in which only husband and wife can be cotenants and neither (alone) can cause a division of the property.

Tenancy in common: A form of joint ownership in which two or more persons own the same property. At the death of a tenant-in-common, ownership transfers to that person's designated beneficiaries or heirs, not to the other joint owner.

Testamentary disposition: Property disposed of by will.

Testamentary trust: A trust set up in a will that only takes effect after death.

Testate: Having left a valid will.

Testator: The individual who creates a will.

Total return: Price appreciation or depreciation of the principal value of an investment plus dividend income of interest.

Totten trust: Also known as a "payable-on-death" (POD) account; a way to leave a bank account to a beneficiary named when the account was opened.

Transfer agent: A corporate representative (or employee) who transfers ownership of a corporation's stock and/or bonds from one person to another; transfer agents are used by executors, administrators, trustors, trustees, guardians, and conservators when changing title on a security.

Trust: A legal arrangement in which one person (the trustor) transfers legal title to property to a trust and names a fiduciary (the trustee) to manage the property for the benefit of a person or institution (the beneficiary).

Trustee: The person or institution who manages property according to the instructions in the trust agreement.

Trustor: The individual who establishes a trust; also referred to as the "settlor" or the "grantor."

Undivided interest: A share of property that has not been physically set aside or divided, such as a joint interest in a home.

Unified tax credit: The estate and gift tax credit of up to $192,800 that permits the transfer of up to $600,000 free of federal estate and gift tax.

Uniform Gifts to Minors Act (UGMA): A federal law that permits you to make gifts to minor children at favorable tax rates.

Unitrust: A charitable remainder trust that provides the donor a fluctuating annual income based on investment performance.

Unlimited marital deduction: Allows a spouse to transfer all property to his or her spouse without federal estate tax.

Vest: To grant immediate and full ownership rights.

Will: A legally binding document directing the disposition of one's property, which is not operative until death and can be revoked up to time of death or until there is a loss of mental capacity to make a valid will.

Yield: The annual rate of return received on an investment.

Index

About the Author

Martin R. Dunetz has been a financial economist for many years, concentrating in investment, retirement, and estate planning. He has received bachelor's, master's, and doctor's degrees; has taught and written for several publications; and is the author of *How to Finance Your Retirement*, published by Prentice-Hall. Dr. Dunetz currently resides in Washington, D.C., with his wife, Marta.